American Literature: A Beginner's Anthology
edited by Daniil Ozernyi

Contents

Supplementary Reading

AF414920

American literature is unique. It is unique primarily due to the historical circumstances which surrounded its dawn. Bringing with them British, Dutch, French, and Spanish heritage, European people came to the new continent and, joined by Native Americans, evolved to form a new literature.

Ever since, the distinct features of American writers were unconditional freedom, fight for ability to express themselves, as well as expose the society in ways which challenge the former. While embarking on a first voyage through these writings, it is vitally important to remember these essentials. As a reader, one faces a need to feel – not to just read and hear – what are the feelings expressed by the author.

However, the question of the author is another important one. It is often postulated that the author has authority to give meaning to the work, and also that there are "right" and "wrong" interpretations of a work of literary merit. I say it is not so.

A reader has ultimate authority over a work's meaning. A Florida high-schooler will always understand a poem in a different manner that a Yale professor. This is unchangeable because our understanding of literature is based on our life experiences. Here's what I tend to think of the authors generally: "the author is not an identity which is expressed through writing and which is superior to the writing. Instead, the writer is "born" with the writing - just like the experience of the reader is born while reading. The reader, finally, receives the same kind of dereference the author does and can interpret the work however their experiences and background direct them."[1]

I hope that, against all odds created by the long-standing tradition, every reader will be able to spring free from the authoritarian nature of "right interpretation", and thus find something personal and intimate in every work which this anthology contains.

---

[1] Ozernyi, D. (2019). *In search for the lost connection: Hierarchical tensions as a unified way of deriving meaning.* International Journal of Social Sciences & Educational Studies, 6(2), 102-108. doi:http://dx.doi.org/10.23918/ijsses.v6i2p102

Always remember: it is your responsibility as readers to examine the work closely, and take it apart, like a canvas, to see what it is composed of, and which of those threads appeal to you personally and intimately. This is when American literature will reveal its beauty and diversity to you.

The United States of America, being 'a melting pot of nations' has developed a really unique literature, which underwent the influence of the literary traditions of a number of ethnic groups inhabiting the country, not only of European and Asian ancestry, but also of Native American and African American origin.

Indigenous people lived in what is now the United States of America for thousands of years before the European colonization. There were about 500 tribes of Native Americans, which had their own languages, religious beliefs, culture, customs, art, and folklore. There had been no communication between the North-American Indians and the rest of the world. Their development was at a low level: they had not even discovered the use of the wheel. They hunted and fished, and were practically unfamiliar with agriculture. They met the early colonists with hospitality. They were eager to trade with the pale-faces, as they called the white men. But when the Indians were cheated and plundered, they began to answer the invaders with blood and fire. Their folk art influenced the further development of American culture.

Scandinavian sailors reached the Western Hemisphere in the 10th century, but there is little evidence of those voyages. The actual discovery of America was made in the 16th century. On October 12, 1492, in search of a shorter and safer trade-route from Europe to Asia, Christopher Columbus landed on an island near Cuba, which he mistook for India. The misunderstanding was cleared up a few years later, when Amerigo Vespucci from Florence explored that coast and found that it was not India. So the new continent was called America after him.

More than a century was spent on exploring both Americas. North America was first explored by a Bristol merchant John Cabot and his son Sebastian, then by Henry Hudson, an English navigator, who was the first to discover what is now the Hudson River. South America was explored by the Spaniards and the Portuguese. At first the only aim of these adventurers was to get gold. That is why they were more interested in the southern part of the continent: there lived numerous rich tribes of Indians, some of them highly civilized. Eventually Spanish settlements appeared in the south, on the Haiti and Cuba.

Real colonization of America started at the beginning of the 17th century. Four European nations competed in that overseas expansion: Spain, Holland, France and England. The English fought for the new territories against the Dutch (1672-1674), the

French and the Spanish (1756-1763). After that, a vast territory was under the English rule. Besides, there was a constant struggle against the Indian tribes. Colonization of America on a large scale in the 17th century was due to the changing conditions in Europe. Hundreds of thousands of poor peasants who had lost their land were forced to leave their native countries and search for new homes across the Atlantic.

In November 1620, a group of English Puritans on board a ship called the *Mayflower* arrived in America and called the place New England. They are called the *Pilgrim Fathers*. 102 people survived that voyage: 78 men and 24 women. They wanted to build up a new society of free people in this new land. Their first winter in the new country was extremely hard as they did not have enough time to build houses and store some food. The local Indians helped them survive, and in the spring they provided them with seeds, so that the new-comers could plant and grow some crops. In the autumn of 1621, having gathered the first harvest, the colonists decided to have a festive dinner to thank God, each other and the Indians for helping them survive that hard period. This is where the tradition of celebrating Thanksgiving comes from.

The settlements of New England developed rapidly. Ten years after the arrival of the Mayflower Pilgrims, more than twenty thousand people lived in the colony, and the majority were from England. And it was here that the literature of the new American nation appeared.

In 1636, the Mayflower Pilgrims founded Harvard College, the first American university. They also set up the first printing press and published the first books. Many of the Pilgrim Fathers had a University education, they brought books on various subjects to America. They opened schools for children.

More and more immigrants arrived in the New World. They drove the Indians from their hunting grounds, established vast plantations on these lands, and they needed help to cultivate them. So, slave trade originated. At first the planters tried to capture and use the Indians, but they never made good slaves: they just could not live in captivity and died; besides, they could easily escape as they knew the country very well. (The Indian Wars eventually ended the Native American slave trade by 1750.) So, the planters began to look for other sources of work-force. They used convicts from prisons in Europe; poor peasants, unable to pay their way to America and ready to risk everything in order to save their families from starvation; kidnapped children from European ports. In 1619, a Dutch ship, the *Treasurer* arrived with the first twenty black slaves from Africa in chains; there followed plenty of others, and slavery flourished.

Task 1. Find out the names of some Indian tribes to present in class and to compare with others. Task 2. Search for some additional information as to the life of the Indians in the past and nowadays. Task 3. Try to discover some facts about the Scandinavian pre-Columbian voyages to America.

Task 4. Find out what places in both Americas are named after their early explorers.

Task 5. Disclose the causes of a large-scale colonization of America in the 17th century and show which country captured which territory. Make a map.

Task 6. Find out more information about the Pilgrim Fathers' arrival in America and their further life. Task 7. What do you know about slavery in America and its abolition?

The Early Colonial Period and the War of Independence

Pocahontas (c.1596-1617) was a Native American woman notable for her association with the colonial settlement at Jamestown, Virginia, which was the first English settlement founded in 1607. She was captured by the English and held for ransom. However, when the opportunity appeared for her to return to her people, she chose to remain with the English. She married the tobacco planter John Rolfe and gave birth to the son Thomas. The family travelled to London, and Pocahontas was presented to English society. Her story has been romanticized over the years, and she has been a subject of art, literature and films.

The representatives of the *early colonial period* in American literature are *William Bradford* (1590- 1657), who was one of the Pilgrim Fathers and wrote a historical book about their arrival; *Anne Bradstreet* (1612-1672), a woman poet born in England, who described the life of the first generation of New Englanders; *Sarah Kemble Knight* (1636-1727), a writer born in America, who kept a school in Boston and once made a long and dangerous trip to New York on horseback, which she described in her diary.

When the British government introduced new taxes without the colonists' approval, they decided to fight for their rights. After the *Boston Tea Party* (1773) American patriots aimed at formation of the new, independent nation out of the separate colonies.

The War of Independence, or *the Revolutionary War* (1775-1783) began in April 1775 with the first armed conflict between England and America. On July 4, 1776, the colonists declared themselves a Democratic Republic and issued the Declaration of Independence. In 1789, they adopted the Constitution of the young country. There were thirteen original colonies in this new union (Massachusetts, New Hampshire, Rhode Island, Connecticut, New York, New Jersey, Pennsylvania, Delaware, Maryland, Virginia, North Carolina, South Carolina, and Georgia). However, the war continued till 1783.

Enlightenment in America, or the *Age of Reason*, was closely connected with the War of Independence and represented by Benjamin Franklin, Thomas Jefferson, Thomas Paine and Philip Freneau. Their main aim was to spread the republican ideas among the people and defend the rights of man. People wanted to share their ideas with their fellow-countrymen. The result was a tremendous development of journalism. The interest in science and education increased greatly.

Benjamin Franklin (1706-1790) was a figure of universal dimensions. He was a printer, writer, philosopher, scientist, economist, and statesman. As one of the leaders of the Revolution, he participated in the most important events of his time. He was born in Boston, Massachusetts, the youngest of seventeen children in the family of a poor English immigrant. At the age of seventeen, he went to New York, but could not find employment there, so he went to Philadelphia which became his home. In 1724, he went to Britain to master the technique of printing. Later, he started a periodical, and then experimented on electricity and lightning. As a statesman, he was sent to England to defend the interests of the colonies. Together with Thomas Jefferson he prepared the text of the Declaration of Independence, and later, the Constitution. He managed to get a financial aid from France and convinced the European people to recognize the young American Republic. He wrote the Autobiography, which was intended for his sons and grandsons rather than for the world, but it was published after his death and was widely read.

American English

In the 17th century the New Englanders in the North, as well as the Virginians in the South spoke the language of Shakespeare and Milton. It was the London dialect, which in the 16th century in Britain was the model language for cultured Englishmen and was accepted as standard English. But in America this language suffered a change. Moreover, there developed several dialects as there was little contact between the colonies. A decisive step towards the development of a single language was the formation of the United States as a result of the Revolutionary War.

There are three types of words called *Americanisms* – the new words and word combinations, which appeared in American English and have not been accepted in Britain.

1.	The names of plants, animals etc, which were unfamiliar to the immigrants, and they either borrowed the Indian names (raccoon, moose, caucus, pow-wow, wigwam) or invented their own,

e.g. live-oak – an evergreen tree, back-country – lands far from Indians; groundhog, egg-plant, sweet potato, cat-bird, bull-frog, sun-fish.

2.	Archaisms. These are words and phrases that have become out of use in England, but survived in America, e.g. I guess – I suppose, mad – angry, fall – autumn, pass – die, gotten – got, sick – ill.

3.	Words borrowed from other European languages and African American slaves. From Dutch: boss, cookie, stoop, spook, hamburger, noodle, dollar; French: bureau, gopher, depot; Spanish: canyon, mesa, rodeo, ranch, lasso, sombrero; German: pretzel; Negro: banjo.

Some words are just different in British and American English: Br.E. sweets – Am.E. candy; flat – apartment; biscuits – cookies; I haven't got – I don't have, lift – elevator, railway – railroad.

There are also some differences in spelling, e.g. Br.E. centre, theatre – Am.E. center, theater; colour, neighbour – color, neighbor; traveller, travelling – traveler, traveling; programme – program etc.

A number of words originated in American English, but are now used in British, too: blizzard, deadline, gangster, hijack, know-how, T-shirt, teenager, workaholic, parole, scientist, awful, cocktail, belittle.

American literature of the first half of the 19th century. Romanticism.

The literary current of Romanticism appeared in America as

the result of the Revolutionary War. It was also caused by the disappointment of the democratic minded people in the social situation in the country: the contradictions between the rich and the poor were dramatic, Negro slavery flourished, the Indian tribes were exterminated. On the other hand, it was the time when new lands were discovered.

Romanticism brought about the first important works of American poetry and fiction. The writers of this period depicted life as a struggle between virtue and evil, and insisted that good should defeat bad. They produced a powerful literature with wide variations. They developed such genres as the novel (historical, social, fantastic), the romance and the short story. They gave their readers a taste for old ballads, epics and the folk-tales of the Indians. Nature was one of the major themes for American romanticists. In romanticist literature a reader finds a complicated plot, dynamic development of the events and sudden changes in the fates of the heroes.

The writers of romanticism were true patriots: they loved their country and recognized the importance of developing national literature and glorifying national history.

Flourishing from the 1820s till the 1850s, romanticism can be divided into early romanticism (the 1820s and 1830s) and late romanticism (the 1840s and 1850s).

Task 1. Find out more about Pocahontas and the folk tales about her to share in class.

Task 2. Tell your classmates about the Boston Tea Party, its causes and consequences.

Task 3. Share information from your history lessons about the American Revolutionary War.

Task 4. Why was Benjamin Franklin so important in American history?

Task 5. Give your own examples of Americanisms and other differences from British English.

Task 6. Describe the social situation, which led to the appearance of Romanticism. Write a short essay.

Washington Irving

(April 3, 1783, – November 28, 1859)

Irving was called the "first American man of letters." He was a famous short story writer, essayist, biographer, historian, and diplomat.

The youngest of 11 children in the family of a prosperous Scottish merchant in New York, Irving grew up in an atmosphere of indulgence. Being sickly in childhood, he was not sent to school and was educated at home. He escaped a college education, which his father required of his older sons. However, at the age of 17 he began studying law in the office of Josiah Hoffman, with whose pretty daughter Matilda he fell in love.

Irving made his literary debut in 1802, when he published a series of satirical essays under the pseudonym of Jonathan Oldstyle, Gent.. He made several trips up the Hudson, then to Canada for the sake of his health. An extended tour of Europe in 1804–1806 stimulated his interest in foreign culture. On his return, he passed the bar examination and started a career of a lawyer. Irving's creative

activity can be divided into three periods: early American, European, and late American.

A History of New York, from the Beginning of the World to the End of the Dutch Dynasty, by Diedrich Knickerbocker (1809) was a comic history of the Dutch rule in New York, prefaced by a satirical account of the world from creation onward. Its writing was interrupted in April 1809 by the sudden death of Matilda Hoffman. His grief was great, and his life seemed aimless for some years.

In 1815, he went to Europe and spent the following 17 years there, visiting different countries. In London, he met Sir Walter Scott, who encouraged him to renew his literary efforts. The result was *The Sketch Book of Geoffrey Crayon, Gent.* (1820), a collection of stories and essays that mix satire and whimsicality with fact and fiction. Among them were the tales *The Legend of Sleepy Hollow* and *Rip Van Winkle*, which are considered the first American short stories. They are both Americanized versions of German folktales. *The Legend of Sleepy Hollow* was inspired by the numerous tales about a headless horseman. The main character of *Rip Van Winkle* sleeps for 20 years in the mountains and awakes as an old man to find his wife dead, his daughter happily married, and America an independent country. The tremendous success of *The Sketch Book* in both England and the United States assured Irving that he could live by his pen. In 1822, he produced *Bracebridge Hall*, a sequel to *The Sketch Book*. He travelled in Germany, Austria, France, Spain, the British Isles, and later in his own country.

Irving was interested in folklore. He collected tales, legends, and stories (about robbers, ghosts, mysteries) to use their plots in his own creations. By restoring the tales of the past, he wanted to cure the modern world by wisdom. Thus, the short story *The Devil and Tom Walker* is based on an old German legend about a man who sold his soul to the devil. This tale was later used by Goethe in his play *Faust*.

After a 17-year absence, Irving returned to New York in 1832, where he was warmly received. He made a journey west and produced in rapid succession *A Tour of the Prairies* (1835), *Astoria* (1836), and *The Adventures of Captain Bonneville* (1837). Irving also wrote biographies of some famous people, among them – Christopher Columbus and George Washington. Except for four years (1842 – 1846) as minister to Spain, Irving spent the rest of his life at his home, "Sunnyside," in Tarrytown, on the Hudson River, where he devoted himself to writing.

Task 1. Make up a chronological table of Irving's life and literary activity to discuss with your partner in class.

Task 2. Find out the content of one of Irving's works to exchange with your classmates in groups. Task 3. Discuss Irving's place and significance in American literature as a class.

From *The Legend of Sleepy Hollow* by Washington Irving

...From the listless repose of this place, and the peculiar character of its inhabitants, who are descendants from the original Dutch settlers, this sequestered glen has long been known by the name of SLEEPY HOLLOW, and its rustic lads are called the Sleepy Hollow Boys throughout all the neighboring country. A drowsy, dreamy influence seems to hang over the land, and to pervade the very atmosphere. Some say that the place was bewitched by a High German doctor, during the early days of the settlement; others, that an old Indian chief, the prophet or wizard of his tribe, held his powwows there before the country was discovered by Master Hendrick Hudson.

The dominant spirit, however, that haunts this enchanted region, and seems to be commander-in-chief of all the powers of the air, is the apparition of a figure on horseback, without a head. It is said by some to be the ghost of a Hessian trooper, whose head had been carried away by a cannon-ball, in some nameless battle during the Revolutionary War, and who is ever and anon seen by the country folk hurrying along in the gloom of night, as if on the wings of the wind. His haunts are not confined to the valley, but extend at times to the adjacent roads, and especially to the vicinity of a church at no great distance. Indeed, certain of the most authentic historians of those parts, who have been careful in collecting and collating the floating facts concerning this spectre, allege that the body of the trooper having been buried in the churchyard, the ghost rides forth to the scene of battle in nightly quest of his head, and that the rushing speed with which he sometimes passes along the Hollow, like a midnight blast, is owing to his being belated, and in a hurry to get back to the churchyard before daybreak.

... Ichabod, who had no relish for this strange midnight companion, and bethought himself of the adventure of Brom Bones with the Galloping Hessian, now quickened his steed in hopes of leaving him behind. The stranger, however, quickened his horse to an equal pace. Ichabod pulled up, and fell into a walk, thinking to lag behind, – the other did the same. His heart began to sink within him... On mounting a rising ground, which brought the figure of his fellow-traveller in relief against the sky, gigantic in height, and muffled in a cloak, Ichabod was horror-struck on perceiving that he was headless! – but his horror was still more increased on observing that the head, which should have rested on his shoulders, was carried before him on the pommel of his saddle! His terror rose to desperation; he rained a shower of kicks and blows upon Gunpowder, hoping by a sudden movement to give his companion the slip; but the spectre started full jump with him. Away, then, they dashed through thick and thin; stones flying and sparks flashing at every bound.

... The next morning the old horse was found without his saddle, and with the bridle under his feet, soberly cropping the grass at his master's gate. Ichabod did not make his appearance at breakfast; dinner- hour came, but no Ichabod. The boys assembled at the schoolhouse, and strolled idly about the banks of the brook; but no schoolmaster. Hans Van Ripper now began to feel some uneasiness about the fate of poor Ichabod, and his saddle. An inquiry was set on foot, and after diligent investigation they came upon his traces. In one part of the road leading to the church was found the saddle trampled in the dirt; the tracks of horses' hoofs deeply dented in the road, and evidently at furious speed, were traced to the bridge, beyond which, on the bank of a broad part of the brook, where the water ran deep and black, was found the hat of the unfortunate Ichabod, and close beside it a shattered pumpkin. The brook was searched, but the body of the schoolmaster was not to be discovered...

Task 1. Make a list of the words, which help describe the place vividly, and compare them in pairs. Task 2. Can you spot any historic facts or names in the extract? Share your findings in class.

Task 3. What literary means help create the bright picture of the competition between the man and the ghost? Write out the corresponding words and compare them as a class. Use them in your own sentences.

Task 4. Can we infer any events of that night race from the facts given? What are they? Search for the ending of the story and write your own to share in class.

James Fenimore Cooper

(September 15, 1789 – September 14, 1851)

Cooper was the creator of the American novel, greatly influenced by the ideas of the age of Enlightenment; he wanted to see his people live by humane and democratic principles.

Cooper was born in Burlington, New Jersey, the eleventh of twelve children in the family of a judge. Soon his family moved to the state of New York, the place now called Cooperstown. The children were educated at the village school and at home, but they learnt a lot from outdoor life. Young Cooper was very skilled in outdoor activities, but read very little. His early experiences in this frontier town on the border of wilderness gave him the background knowledge used in the *Pioneers* (1923). After finishing the boarding school in Albany, Cooper attended Yale College from 1803 till 1805, but

was expelled because of a misbehaviour. In 1806, he became a sailor and then a midshipman in the Navy. At twenty, he inherited a fortune from his father, married Susan Augusta De Lancey and became a country gentleman, devoting himself to his family of seven children.

Cooper began writing at the age of thirty. National American literature had just started developing, and there was a great need for a talented writer to record for future generations the heroic past of the country. Cooper managed to cope with this task. He left a very large literary heritage. In addition to his 32 novels, he wrote a history of the US Navy and a lot of articles and pamphlets on social problems.

In 1820, Cooper's wife persuaded him that he could write a book better than the one she was reading. What followed was *Precaution* (1820), a novel of morals and manners that showed the influence of Jane Austen. The book was received warmly, and he soon published *The Spy: A Tale of Neutral Ground* (1821), the first historical romance about the American Revolution. Its success inspired him to write another book, *The Pioneers* (1923), which was the first in a series of five books about Natty Bumppo, called *The Leatherstocking Tales*: *The Last of the Mohicans* (1826), *The Prairie* (1927), *The Pathfinder* (1940), *The Deerslayer* (1941). Thus, he created the first American novel and hero. He also brought up the thematical complexities of natural right versus legal right, order versus change, and wilderness versus civilization.

In 1826, at the height of his popularity, Cooper sailed to Europe together with his large family for a seven-year tour. He travelled and worked all the time, and wrote seven novels, a lot of articles, essays and letters. He was nicknamed "the American Scott" because of the style of his historical novels, which was like that of Sir Walter Scott.

Returning to the US in 1833, Cooper was greatly disappointed by the changes which had happened there. Thousands of people had left their homes and rushed west to take the lands from the Indians; industrialization and banking were developing. Cooper could not help expressing his criticism as to this new order. His critical works were misunderstood on both continents. Nevertheless, Cooper continued to write the series about Natty Bumppo – a white man, a hunter, who was just and kind, and knew a lot about forest life. He said that all men, white, black, yellow or red, were brothers; he was against civilization because he thought it spoilt nature and people. The Indians were closer to Natty Bumppo than the white civilized Americans; when he became old, he joined one of the Indian tribes.

Then came Cooper's obsession with the sea from his previous experience in the Navy. He wrote *The History of the Navy of the United States of America* (1839), *The Cruise of Sommers* (1844), and *The Distinguished American Naval Officers* (1846). At the end of his life Cooper was more successful and respected abroad than at home. Nowadays, it is difficult to find a person who has not read a book or seen a film about brave Indians, the noble and wise Natty Bumppo, and beautiful American nature.

From *The Last of the Mohicans* by James Fenimore Cooper

A young man, in the dress of an officer, conducted to their steeds two females, who, as it was apparent by their dresses, were prepared to encounter the fatigues of a journey in the woods. One, and she was the more juvenile in her appearance, though both were young, permitted glimpses of her dazzling complexion, fair golden hair, and bright blue eyes, to be caught, as she artlessly suffered the morning air to blow aside the green veil which descended low from her beaver.

The flush which still lingered above the pines in the western sky was not more bright nor delicate than the bloom on her cheek; nor was the opening day more cheering than the animated smile which she bestowed on the youth, as he assisted her into the saddle. The other, who appeared to share equally in the attention of the young officer, concealed her charms from the gaze of the soldiery with a care that seemed better fitted to the experience of four or five additional years. It could be seen, however, that her person, though molded with the same exquisite proportions, of which none of the graces were lost by the traveling dress she wore, was rather fuller and more mature than that of her companion.

No sooner were these females seated, than their attendant sprang lightly into the saddle of the war- horse, when the whole three bowed to Webb, who in courtesy, awaited their parting on the threshold of his cabin and turning their horses' heads, they proceeded at a slow amble, followed by their train, toward the northern entrance of the encampment. As they traversed that short distance, not a voice was heard among them; but a slight exclamation proceeded from the younger of the females, as the Indian runner glided by her, unexpectedly, and led the way along the military road in her front. Though this sudden and startling movement of the Indian produced no sound from the other, in the surprise her veil also was allowed to open its folds, and betrayed an indescribable look of pity, admiration, and horror, as her dark eye followed the easy motions of the savage. The tresses of this lady were shining and black, like the plumage of the raven. Her complexion was not brown, but it rather appeared charged with the color of the rich blood, that seemed ready to burst its bounds. And yet there was neither coarseness nor want of shadowing in a countenance that was exquisitely regular, and dignified and surpassingly beautiful. She smiled, as if in pity at her own momentary forgetfulness, discovering by the act a row of teeth that would have shamed the purest ivory; when, replacing the veil, she bowed her face, and rode in silence, like one whose thoughts were abstracted from the scene around her.

...While one of the lovely beings we have so cursorily presented to the reader was thus lost in thought, the other quickly recovered from the alarm which induced the exclamation, and, laughing at her own weakness, she inquired of the youth who rode by her side:

"Are such specters frequent in the woods, Heyward, or is this sight an especial entertainment ordered on our behalf? If the latter, gratitude must close our mouths; but if the former, both Cora and I shall have need to draw largely on that stock of hereditary courage which we boast..."

"That Indian is a 'runner' of the army; and, after the fashion of his people, he may be accounted a hero," returned the officer. "He has volunteered to guide us to the lake, by a path but little known, sooner than if we followed the tardy movements of the column; and, by consequence, more agreeably."

"I like him not," said the lady, shuddering, partly in assumed, yet more in real terror. "You know him, Duncan, or you would not trust yourself so freely to his keeping?"

"Say, rather, Alice, that I would not trust you. I do know him, or he would not have my confidence..."

Task 1. Make up a table of Cooper's life and literary activity to help your presentation in class. Task 2. Get ready to retell the content of one of Cooper's novels to your younger sibling.

Task 3. Define the words which help the author describe the appearance of the two girls; make a list. Task 4. Spot the peculiarities of the characters' speech in the dialogue; note useful expressions.

Task 5. Watch the film based on this book and compare it with the original in a class discussion.

Edgar Allan Poe

(January 19, 1809 – October 7, 1849)

Poe was an outstanding American Romantic writer, poet, editor and critic, one of the first professional writers in the USA, who had a profound influence on world literature. He is considered the creator of horror, detective and science fiction and the architect of the modern short story. He has also been seen as a forerunner to the "art for art's sake" movement. His works have been translated into many languages and retain their popularity even now. In America, there is the *Edgar Award* for distinguished works in the mystery genre.

Poe was born in Boston, Massachusetts. His parents, poor professional actors, died before the boy was three years old, and he was brought up by a childless couple, John and Frances Allan from Richmond, Virginia. His foster mother

loved him very much and understood his aspirations. However, his father, a prosperous Scotch tobacco merchant, never understood his son's feelings and his vocation for art. The boy attended the best boarding schools. He was really talented both in sports and arts. From 1815 to 1820, the family lived in Scotland and England, and Poe attended a fine classical school, where he wrote Latin verses and learned boxing. Back in the United States, he was sent to the University of Virginia, where Poe did well in mathematics, chemistry and medicine. He read a lot and started writing poetry himself. However, disliking the studied subjects, he did not feel happy and started drinking and gambling. Less than in a year he was forced to leave the university.

Poe returned briefly to Richmond, but his relationship with father became even worse. Mr Allan made him a clerk in his business, and Poe immediately ran away. In 1827, he moved to Boston and enlisted in the United States Army. His first collection of poems, *Tamerlane, and Other Poems*, was published in Boston that same year. Within a year, he could not stand army life any more, so he left it. In 1829, he published in Baltimore his second collection entitled *Al Aaraaf, Tamerlane, and Minor Poems*. Both volumes passed unnoticed. Following his Army service, Poe was admitted to the United States Military Academy in West Point, but he was again forced to leave for disobeying orders and lack of financial support. Mr Allan refused to help him any longer, and he did not mention him in his will. So, when he died in two years' time, Poe got nothing. In 1831, Poe published his third collection of poems, this time in New York. However, he first became famous not as a poet, but as a writer of fiction, with the story *MS (manuscript) Found in a Bottle*. He won a prize of fifty dollars for it that saved him from starvation and opened the way into journalism. He then moved into the home of his aunt Maria Clemm and her daughter Virginia in Baltimore, Maryland.

Poe began to sell short stories to magazines at around this time, and, in 1835, he became the editor of the Southern Literary Messenger in Richmond, where he moved with his aunt and cousin Virginia. He published his old and new tales and poems in this magazine. He wrote a lot of book reviews, which won popularity for the magazine. In 1836, Poe married Virginia, who was fourteen years old at that time. They were very happy, but soon she fell ill with tuberculosis. Poe had no money to cure her. He was desperate and took to drinking. Over the next ten years, Poe edited a number of literary journals in Philadelphia and in New York City. It was during these years that he established himself as a poet, a short story writer, and an editor. He published some of his best-known stories and poems, including *The Gold Bug* (1843), collection of poetry *The Raven and Other Poems* (1845), *The Black Cat, The Fall of the House of Usher, The Tell-Tale Heart, The Murders in the Rue Morgue, The Mystery of Marie Roget, Eldorado, The Bells, Annabel Lee*. Altogether, he wrote about 60 stories and 48 poems. However, he was more popular in Europe than at home.

After Virginia's death in 1847, Poe felt really depressed. In two years, he died in Baltimore.

From *The Gold-Bug* by Edgar Allan Poe

"...I now scrutinized the death's-head with care. Its outer edges – the edges of the drawing nearest the edge of the vellum – were far more distinct than the others. It was clear that the action of the caloric had been imperfect or unequal. I immediately kindled a fire, and subjected every portion of the parchment to a glowing heat. At first, the only effect was the strengthening of the faint lines in the skull; but, upon persevering in the experiment, there became visible, at the corner of the slip, diagonally opposite to the spot in which the death's-head was delineated, the figure of what I at first supposed to be a goat. A closer scrutiny, however, satisfied me that it was intended for a kid."

"Ha! ha!" said I, "to be sure I have no right to laugh at you – a million and a half of money is too serious a matter for mirth – but you are not about to establish a third link in your chain – you will not find any especial connection between your pirates and a goat – pirates, you know, have nothing to do with goats; they appertain to the farming interest."

"But I have just said that the figure was not that of a goat."

"Well, a kid then – pretty much the same thing."

"Pretty much, but not altogether," said Legrand. "You may have heard of one *Captain* Kidd. I at once looked upon the figure of the animal as a kind of punning or hieroglyphical signature. I say signature; because its position upon the vellum suggested this idea. The death's-head at the corner diagonally opposite, had, in the same manner, the air of a stamp, or seal. But I was sorely put out by the absence of all else – of the body to my imagined instrument – of the text for my context."

"I presume you expected to find a letter between the stamp and the signature..."

Task 1. Get ready for a class discussion about the causes of Poe's works' ever-lasting popularity. Task 2. Make up a bar graph of Poe's life and literary activity to help your presentation in class. Task 3. Find interesting lexis in the above quoted works; analyse its role in pairs; deliver the results. Task 4. Learn two of the poems by heart and get ready for the reciting contest.

Task 5. Find some translations of the Poe's works and compare them with the original. Task 6. Draw a picture illustrating one of Poe's works and present it in class.

Henry Wadsworth Longfellow

(February 27, 1807 – March 24, 1882)

Longfellow was a famous American scholar, novelist and poet, who won recognition all over the world. Many universities awarded him with honorary degrees. He was a member of the Academies of Sciences of different countries. His work was admired by Queen Victoria and her husband Prince Alfred, Prime Minister William Gladstone, poets Lord Alfred Tennyson and Walt Whitman, and Oscar Wilde. Longfellow is the only American poet whose bust is in Westminster Abbey's Poets' Corner.

Longfellow was born in Portland, Maine, on the Atlantic coast, in the family of a well-to-do lawyer. The family kept alive the memory of the War of Independence, and as a boy Longfellow was told about the heroic deeds of his grandfather, a general in Washington's army, and about his uncle Henry, an officer in the US

Navy, killed in 1804 while defending his country. The family traditions of heroism played a great role in the life of the young boy.

Henry attended a private school and then Bowdoin College, in Maine. There he wrote his first verses and stories. Among his fellow students was the writer, Nathaniel Hawthorne. Longfellow was an excellent student, showing proficiency in foreign languages. Upon graduation in 1825, he was offered a position to teach modern languages at Bowdoin, but on the condition that he should first travel to Europe, at his own expense, to research the languages. He spent three years in England, France, Spain, Italy and Germany, studying languages and literature. There he developed a lifelong love of the Old World civilizations.

In 1829, Longfellow returned home, got married and started teaching. Because the study of foreign languages was so new in America, Longfellow had to write his own textbooks. Also, in 1835, he published his first book *Outre-Mer: A Pilgrimage beyond the Sea*, a collection of travel essays on his European experience. In 1834, he was offered a professorship at Harvard University in Cambridge, Massachusetts.

Before he began working at Harvard, Longfellow and his wife

traveled to Europe, where he studied German, Dutch and Danish literatures to qualify himself. In 1836, while in Germany, his wife died. Devastated, Longfellow came back to the United States and turned to writing, seeking consolation. Later on, in 1843, he married Frances Appleton and they had six children.

Over the next 15 years, Longfellow created his best works such as *Voices of the Night* (1939), a collection of poems including *Hymn to the Night* and *A Psalm of Life*, which gained him immediate popularity, and the novel *Hyperion* (1839). Other publications followed such as *Ballads and Other Poems* (1841), containing *The Wreck of the Hesperus* and the *Village Blacksmith*. His literary activity was influenced by Romanticism. During this time, Longfellow also taught full time at Harvard and directed the Modern Languages Department. He himself knew twelve modern foreign languages, as well as ancient Greek, Latin, Gothic, Hebrew, old French and German.

After the third trip to Europe Longfellow published his masterpiece, a collection of verses *Poems on Slavery* (1842). His philosophical lyrics were very popular in the 1850s and 1860s, among them the poem *The Building of the Ship*. In his mature years Longfellow created beautiful lyrics about nature, which came to life under his pen. He was especially skilful in depicting the seasons of the year.

Longfellow sympathized with common labourers, white and black, and Indians. As a student he began to collect Indian folklore, and later on, he created his epic poem *The Song of Hiawatha* (1855).

Within 39 years he translated the works of different times and peoples – *The Poets and Poetry of Europe* (31 volumes). After his wife's death in 1861, he started translating Dante's *The Divine Comedy*. The same year, the Civil War broke out, and his son Charlie went off to fight without father's approval. Longfellow devoted all his time to his work. His literary legacy still enjoys great popularity in the world.

Thomas Mayne Reid
(April 4, 1818 – October 22, 1883)

Reid was a Scots-Irish American novelist. He wrote many adventure novels like those written by Robert Louis Stevenson. These novels are set primarily in exotic places: the American West, Mexico, South Africa, the Himalayas, and Jamaica.

Reid was born in the north of Ireland, the son of a church clerk. His father wanted him to become a Presbyterian minister, so in September 1834 he enrolled at the Royal Belfast Academical Institution. Although he stayed there for four years, he could not motivate himself enough to complete his studies and receive a degree. He headed back home to teach at school.

In December 1839, Reid boarded a ship going to New Orleans, Louisiana, and found a job as a clerk in the corn trade. He stayed there for six months and left his position as a result of his refusal to whip slaves. Then he travelled to Tennessee, where he tutored some children on a plantation and even founded a private school in Nashville.

In late 1842, Reid arrived in Pittsburgh, Pennsylvania, where he began his literary career writing both prose and poetry under the pen-name *The Poor Scholar*. In early 1843, Reid moved to Philadelphia, where he remained for three years. During this time, he worked as a journalist and from time to time had poetry published in different magazines. It was there that he met Edgar Allan Poe and they became friends.

When the Mexican-American War began in 1846, Reid was a correspondent in Newport, Rhode Island. He joined the First New York Volunteer Infantry as a second lieutenant. In January, 1847 the regiment left New York by ship. Using the pseudonym *Ecolier*, Reid was a correspondent for the New York newspaper, *Spirit of the Times*. On September 13, at the Battle of Chapultepec, the young officer received a severe thigh wound. He was afterward promoted to the rank of first lieutenant for bravery in battle. In July, 1848 he returned to New York with his regiment.

Having moved to London, Reid published his first novel *The Rifle Rangers* (1850), followed by *The Scalp Hunters* (1851), *The*

Desert Home (1852), and *The Boy Hunters* (1853). In 1853 he married Elizabeth Hyde, a 15-year-old lady. After a short time off to spend with his bride and honeymoon, he soon returned to writing. Continuing to base his novels on his adventures in America, he published several more successful novels: *The White Chief* (1855), *The Quadroon* (1856), *Oceola* (1858), and *The Headless Horseman* (1865).

In 1867, Reid returned to America and settled in New York. He lectured at Steinway Hall, and published the novel *The Helpless Hand* in 1868. But America was not as kind to Reid this time. The wound he had received at Chapultepec started to bother him, and he was hospitalized for several months in June 1870. Elizabeth did not like America, and after his treatment they returned to England in October, 1870.

Suffering from acute melancholia, he was soon again hospitalized. He tried to write, but completed few projects. He lived mainly off his U.S. Army pension, which was not enough to cover his needs. Reid died in London.

It has been reported that President of the United States Theodore Roosevelt and the famous British writer Arthur Conan Doyle named Mayne Reid their favourite childhood author and major early inspiration.

Task 1. Make a table of Reid's life and literary activity. How was his time distributed between his two motherlands? Make a list of the places where his novels are set, and of their characters.

Task 2. Choose one of Reid's books to retell its content to a younger child.

From *The Headless Horseman* by Mayne Reid

The players spring to their feet, and draw their machetes. Phelim stands a fair chance of being skewered on three long Toledos. He is only saved by a contingency – another interruption that has the effect of staying the intent. Barajo appears in the doorway panting for breath.

It is scarce necessary for him to announce his errand, though he contrives to gasp out – "He is coming – on the bluff already – ... quick, comrades, quick!"

The Galwegian is saved. There is scarce time to kill him – even were it worth while.

But it is not – at least so think the masqueraders; who leave him to resume his disturbed slumber, and rush forth to accomplish the more profitable assassination.

In a score of seconds, they are under the cliff, at the bottom of the sloping gorge by which it must be descended. They take stand under the branches of a spreading cypress; and await the approach of their victim.

They listen for the hoof strokes that should announce it.

These are soon heard. There is the clinking of a shod hoof – not in regular strokes, but as if a horse was passing over an uneven surface.

One is descending the slope!

He is not yet visible to the eyes of the ambuscaders. Even the gorge is in gloom – like the valley below, shadowed by tall trees.

There is but one spot where the moon throws light upon the turf – a narrow space outside the sombre shadow that conceals the assassins. Unfortunately, this does not lie in the path of their intended victim.

He must pass under the canopy of the cypress!

"Don't kill him!" mutters Miguel Diaz to his men, speaking in an earnest tone. "There's no need for that just yet. I want to have him alive – for the matter of an hour or so. I have my reasons. Lay hold of him and his horse. There can be no danger, as he will be taken by surprise, and unprepared. If there be resistance, we must shoot him down; but let me fire first."

The confederates promise compliance. They have soon an opportunity of proving the sincerity of their promise. He for whom they are waiting has accomplished the descent of the slope, and is passing under the shadow of the cypress.

"Down with your weapons! To the ground!" cries El Coyote, rushing forward and seizing the bridle, while the other three fling themselves upon the man who is seated in the saddle.

There is no resistance, either by struggle or blow; no blade drawn; no shot discharged: not even a word spoken in protest!

They see a man standing upright in the stirrups; they lay their hands upon limbs that feel solid flesh and bone, and yet seem insensible to the touch!

The horse alone shows resistance. He rears upon his hind legs, makes ground backward, and draws his captors after him. He carries them into the light, where the moon is shining outside the shadow.

Merciful heaven! what does it mean?

His captors let go their hold, and fall back with a simultaneous shout. It is a scream of wild terror!

Not another instant do they stay under the cypress; but commence retreating at top speed towards the thicket where their own steeds have been left tied.

Mounting in mad haste, they ride rapidly away.

They have seen that which has already stricken terror into hearts more courageous than theirs – *a horseman without a head*!

Task 1. Read the extract and, in pairs, helping each other, describe the scene in your own words, emphasizing the characters' feelings before, during and after the meeting with a stranger.

Task 2. Identify in groups what words and phrases make the description more vivid.

Harriet Beecher-Stowe

Beecher-Stowe (1811-1896) was a representative of the abolition literature, considered part of romantic literature, but with a lot of realistic details. Harriet Elisabeth Beecher was born in Litchfield, Connecticut, in a pastor's family and brought up in the religious atmosphere. She studied at her elder sister's school for girls. In 1832 she moved to Cincinnati, Ohio, not far from Virginia, where the life of slaves was especially hard. She heard a lot of stories of the slave markets, broken Negro families, cruelty of masters.

In 1836, Harriet married Calvin Stowe, a professor of theology, and had four sons and three daughters, but tried to find time for writing. In 1843, her short stories were published in the book *Mayflower*. Her family were against slavery; they supported the Underground Railroad, housing slaves in their home; they then ran north to freedom in Canada. In 1850, her family moved to the state of Maine, and there she began writing the novel *Uncle Tom's Cabin*, which depicted hard conditions for enslaved African Americans. It appeared in 1852 and had a great success. Some critics said that the facts in the book were not true. So, she published another book, *Key to Uncle Tom's Cabin* (1853) – it was a collection of the documents used in her novel.

When the Civil War between the North and the South began in 1861, Beecher-Stowe was proud of her son who was a soldier in the Army of the North. In 1862, President Abraham Lincoln received her at the White House and said, "You are the little lady who wrote the book that started this great war."

After the War, she lived and worked in Florida. She died in Hartford, Connecticut.

From *Uncle Tom's Cabin* by Harriet Beecher Stowe

Late in the afternoon of a chilly day in February, two gentlemen were sitting alone over their wine, in a well-furnished dining parlor, in Kentucky. There were no servants present, and the gentlemen, with chairs closely approaching, seemed to be discussing some subject with great earnestness.

..."That is the way I should arrange the matter," said Mr. Shelby.

"I can't make trade that way – I positively can't, Mr. Shelby," said the other, holding up a glass of wine between his eye and the light.

"Why, the fact is, Haley, Tom is an uncommon fellow; he is certainly worth that sum anywhere, – steady, honest, capable, manages my whole farm like a clock."

"You mean honest, as niggers go," said Haley, helping himself to a glass of brandy.

"No; I mean, really, Tom is a good, steady, sensible, pious fellow. He got religion at a camp-meeting, four years ago; and I believe he really did get it. I've trusted him, since then, with everything I have, – money, house, horses, – and let him come and go round the country; and I always found him true and square in everything."

"Some folks don't believe there are pious niggers Shelby," said Haley...

..."Why, last fall, I let him go to Cincinnati alone, to do business for me, and bring home five hundred dollars. 'Tom,' said I to him, 'I trust you, because I think you're a Christian – I know you wouldn't cheat.' Tom came back, sure enough; I knew he would. Some low fellows, they say, said to him – 'Tom, why don't you make tracks for Canada?' 'Ah, master trusted me, and I couldn't,' – they told me about it. I am sorry to part with Tom, I must say. You ought to let him cover the whole balance of the debt; and you would, Haley, if you had any conscience."

"Well, I've got just as much conscience as any man in business can afford to keep, – just a little, you know," said the trader, jocularly...

Task 1. Find additional information about the writer's life and creative activity to present in class. Task 2. Get acquainted with the content of the novel and retell it to your younger sibling.

Task 3. What is the above mentioned conversation about? What are the two men trying to arrange? Task 4. In what words is Tom described by his master? What is your attitude to the situation?

Task 5. Do you know any other books describing the hard life of American slaves?

American literature of the second half of the 19th century and the beginning of the 20th century

Realism

In the first half of the 19th century the movement for the abolition of slavery began to spread. In spite of the adoption of the law prohibiting further importation of African slaves into the USA, British, Spanish and Dutch ships continued smuggling slaves from Africa to Cuba and Jamaica; from those islands they were transported to the Southern states, and sold. Abolitionists fought against the institution of slavery. The abolition literature is considered part of romantic literature. At the same time, it developed the American social novel by introducing many realistic details about the customs of that time. One of the great representatives of abolitionist literature was **Harriet Beecher-Stowe**, the author of the world-famous novel *Uncle Tom's Cabin*, in which the cruelty of slavery was revealed, thus stimulating struggle against it.

In 1836 **Ralph Waldo Emerson** (1803-1882) started a movement known as *Transcendentalism*. **Nathaniel Hawthorne** (1804-1864) is famous for his masterpiece, *The Scarlet Letter*. He influenced **Herman Melville** (1819-1891) who is notable for the books *Moby-Dick; or, The Whale* and *Billy Budd*. The two greatest poets of this period were **Walt Whitman** (1819-1892) and **Emily Dickinson** (1830-1886). In the first half of the 20th century the famous poets were Wallace Stevens, T.S. Eliot, Robert Frost, Ezra Pound, Hart Crane. The famous novelists were Mark Twain, Henry James (1843-1916), Edith Wharton (1862-1937), Steven Crane (1871-1900), Frank Norris (1870-1902), Gertrude Stein (1874-1946).

Towards the middle of the 19th century, the romantic trend in American literature gave way to new realistic forms. The change was gradual, reflecting the historical development of the country. The North had been becoming more and more industrialized, and the conflict between the interests of the Northern capitalism and the Southern slave-ownership was growing sharper, and finally developed into an open clash

– in the spring of 1861 the *Civil War* broke out. Realism as a trend developed after the Civil War.

Realistic literature considerably differed from the creative activity of the previous writers such as Irving, Cooper and Longfellow. The romanticists wrote about ideal individuals and showed their emotions. The realists understood that people should be shown as a whole. They saw man against the background of social conflicts of the day and explained human feelings in relation to this background.

Among the most outstanding realists of this period were Mark Twain, O. Henry and Jack London. Mark Twain depicted common American people with great sympathy and humour. At the same time, he revealed hypocrisy, cruelty and greed. Jack London and O. Henry created typical characters of American common people – farmers, workers, and revealed the truth of modern life.

American critical realism developed in contact with European realism and under its influence. But it enriched world realism by introducing such problems as social injustice and Negro and Indian question.

Task 1. Find out the names of other abolitionists – writers or politicians – and their historical role.

Task 2. Find some quotations by Ralph Waldo Emerson. Exchange them with your partner and decide together how you can use some of them while discussing any problem (e.g. happiness).

Task 3. Describe the historic situation, which caused the Civil War; find out some details about it. Task 4. Can you name any European realistic writers? What were their main topics?

(to Mark Twain's biography)

Task 1. Make a table of Mark Twain's life and literary activity; use it to retell his biography in pairs.

Task 2. Conduct a survey among your relatives and friends about Mark Twain's books they can easily name. What do they remember about their contents? Compare the results as a group.

Task 3. Find out if there are any films based on Mark Twain's books. Decide on their quality. (to the extract)

Task 1. Who are the main characters in the extract? What are their relationships?

Task 2. How can you characterize Tom judging from the extract? And from the whole book? Task 3. What characteristic features can you identify in aunt Polly's speech?

Task 4. Retell your favourite episode from this book to your younger sibling.

Mark Twain

(born Samuel Longhorne Clemens) (November 30, 1835 – April 21,1910)

Twain was one of America's first and foremost realists and humanists. He was also a great humourist and satirist.

Samuel Clemens was born in the little town of Florida, Missouri, on the banks of the Mississippi River. His family soon moved to a small town Hannibal, Missouri. A lawyer by profession, his father was highly intelligent, but not very successful. His mother was very emotional and had a natural sense of humour. Although the family was not wealthy, the boy and his three siblings had a happy childhood. As a schoolboy, he had a lot of friends and was their leader.

The father died when Samuel was twelve years old and the boy had to earn his own living. For the next

ten years, following the steps of his elder brother, he was an apprentice printer and then a printer both in Hannibal and in New York City.

In 1853, Samuel left home and went to New York, then to Philadelphia. In his childhood he used to dream of becoming a boat pilot, and at 20 he realized his dream. Hoping to find his fortune, he headed for South America. On a riverboat to New Orleans, he met a famous riverboat pilot who promised to teach him his skill for five hundred dollars. After completing his training, Samuel piloted riverboats along the Mississippi for four years. During this time, he became familiar with the towns along the mighty River and became acquainted with the characters who would later inhabit many of his novels. He also got his pen- name Mark Twain at this time. This expression is connected with measuring the depth of the water.

Later on, the young man worked with the gold-miners in California for a year. There he began to write short stories and humorous sketches, and sent them to newspapers. Mark Twain actually began his literary career with the short story *The Celebrated Jumping Frog of Calaveras County,* published in 1865. This story brought him national attention, and he devoted the major part of the rest of his life to literary activity.

In 1866, Mark Twain went to Europe for the first time. His book *The Innocents Abroad* (1869) was a great success. In 1870, the writer married Olivia Langdon and had a happy family life, having a son and three daughters. Having tried many professions, Mark Twain gained the necessary knowledge of life and people and found his favorite job – as a writer. Mark Twain went abroad several times and visited different parts of the world. In addition to *The Adventures of Tom Sawyer (1876)*, some of Twain's most popular and widely read works include the novels *The Prince and the Pauper* (1881), *Life on the Mississippi* (1883), *The Adventures of Huckleberry Finn* (1885), *A Connecticut Yankee in King Arthur's Court* (1889), and *Pudd'nhead Wilson* (1894), as well as collections of short stories and essays, such as *The 1,000,000 Bank- Note and Other Stories* (1893), *The Man That Corrupted Hadleyburg and Other Essays* (1900), and *What Is Man?* (1906). A lot of events and characters were taken by Mark Twain from the real life.

Mark Twain's last work was his autobiography, which he dictated. The first volume of the autobiography, over 736 pages, was published by the University of California in November 2010, 100 years after his death, as the author wished. It soon became an unexpected best seller, making Mark Twain one of a very few authors publishing new best-selling volumes in the 19th, 20th, and 21st centuries.

It is interesting to note that Mark Twain was born in 1835, during the appearance of Haley's Comet, and he died during the next appearance of Haley's Comet, 75 years later.

From *The Adventures of Tom Sawyer* by Mark Twain

"Tom!" No answer. "TOM!"

No answer.

"What's gone with that boy, I wonder? You Tom!" No answer.

The old lady pulled her spectacles down and looked over them about the room; then she put them up and looked out under them. She seldom or never looked THROUGH them for so small a thing as a boy; they were her state pair, the pride of her heart, and were built for "style", not service – she could have seen through a pair of stove-lids just as well. She looked perplexed for a moment, and then said, not fiercely, but still loud enough for the furniture to hear:

"Well, I lay if I get hold of you I'll –"

She did not finish, for by this time she was bending down and punching under the bed with the broom, and so she needed breath to punctuate the punches with. She resurrected nothing but the cat.

"I never did see the beat of that boy!"

She went to the open door and stood in it and looked out among the tomato vines and "jimpson" weeds that constituted the garden. No Tom. So she lifted up her voice at an angle calculated for distance and shouted:

"Y-o-u-u TOM!"

There was a slight noise behind her and she turned just in time to seize a small boy by the slack of his roundabout and arrest his flight.

"There! I might have thought of that closet. What you been doing in there?" "Nothing."

"Nothing! Look at your hands. And look at your mouth. What IS that truck?" "I don't know, aunt."

"Well, I know. It's jam – that's what it is. Forty times I've said if you didn't let that jam alone I'd skin you. Hand me that switch."

The switch hovered in the air – the peril was desperate – "My! Look behind you, aunt!"

The old lady whirled round, and snatched her skirts out of danger. The lad fled on the instant, scrambled up the high board-fence, and disappeared over it.

His aunt Polly stood surprised a moment, and then broke into a gentle laugh.

"Hang the boy, can't I never learn anything? Ain't he played me tricks enough like that for me to be looking out for him by this time? But old fools are the biggest fools there are. Can't learn an old dog new tricks, as the saying is. But my goodness, he never plays them alike, two days, and how is a body to know what's coming?.. I ain't doing my duty by that boy, and that's the Lord's truth, goodness knows. Spare the rod and spile the child, as the Good Book says... He's my own dead sister's boy, poor thing, and I ain't got the heart to lash him, somehow. Every time I let him off, my conscience does hurt me so, and every time I hit him my old heart most breaks... He'll play hookey this evening, and I'll just be obliged to make him work, to-morrow, to punish him. It's mighty hard to make him work Saturdays, when all the boys are having holiday, but he hates work more than he hates anything else, and I've GOT to do some of my duty by him, or I'll be the ruination of the child."

Tom did play hookey, and he had a very good time. He got back home barely in season to help Jim, the small colored boy, saw next-day's wood before supper – at least he was there in time to tell his adventures to Jim while Jim did three-fourth of the work. Tom's younger brother (or rather half-brother) Sid was already through with his part of the work, for he was a quiet boy, and had no adventurous, troublesome ways.

(the real name William Sydney Porter)
(September 11, 1862 – June 5, 1910)

O. Henry is a famous Amercian short story writer, whose works are well known throughout the world; they are noted for their witty language, clever wordplay, and unexpected twisted endings.

Porter was born in Greensboro, North Carolina, in a family of a physician. His mother died from tuberculosis when he was three, and his father spent all his time on various inventions. The boy grew up in his grandmother's home. His aunt, who had a private school, encouraged him to study and to read.

Like many other writers, O. Henry tried different professions before he finally found his calling as a short story writer. He started working in his uncle's drugstore in 1879 and became a licensed pharmacist by the age of 19. He used to make sketches of the people who came to the drugstore, and they liked his drawings.

Porter moved to Texas in 1882 hoping to get rid of a persistent cough. He lived on a sheep ranch and learned bits of Spanish and German. In 1884, he went to the Texan capital Austin. He had an active social life in Austin and was a fine musician, skilled with the guitar and mandolin. Over the next several years, Porter took a number of different jobs, from pharmacy to drafting, journalism, and banking. In 1887, he married Athol Estes, who made a romantic runaway marriage with him when she was only 17, and they had a daughter. In 1891, he began working at the First National Bank of Austin as a teller and book-keeper.

However, banking was not Porter's calling; he was quite careless with his bookkeeping, fired by the bank and charged with embezzlement in 1894. He then worked full-time on his humorous weekly called *The Rolling Stone*, which he started while working at the bank. In 1895 the family moved to Houston and Porter worked in the *Houston Post*. When the trial was appointed in 1896, Porter fled the day before it – first to New Orleans, then to Honduras, with which the USA had no extradition treaty, and lived there for six months. He befriended a notorious train robber there, Al Jennings, who later wrote a book about their friendship. The beginning writer focused on writing *Kings and Cabbages*, his first collection of stories. When he learned his wife was dying of tuberculosis, he returned to Austin to be with his family. He stayed with his wife until her death in

1897 and then was sentenced and spent three years in prison in Ohio from 1898 to 1901. During his jail time, he wrote 14 stories, mainly under the pseudonym O. Henry (from the name of the captain of the prison guard, Orrin Henry, who helped him transfer the stories to freedom to be published). The first story is said to have been written in order to get some money for a Christmas present for his daughter, who stayed with the relatives.

O. Henry's prolific writing period began in 1902 in New York City, where he wrote 381 short stories. His second collection of stories, *The Four Million*, was released in 1906. The stories are set in New York City, and the title is based on the population of the city at that time. The collection contained several short story masterpieces, including *The Gift of the Magi* and *The Cop and the Anthem*. It was followed by *The Trimmed Lamp* (1907), *Heart of the West* (1907), *The Voice of the City* (1908), *Roads of Destiny* (1909).

O. Henry's trademark is his witty, plot-twisting endings, and his warm characterization of the awkward and difficult situations and the creative ways people find to resolve them. *The Gift of the Magi* is a story about a young married couple, short on money, who wish to buy each other Christmas gifts. *The Ransom of Red Chief* is a story about two unfortunate kidnappers that snatch the wrong boy. All of these stories are highly entertaining and they are read for pleasure.

In 1952, Marilyn Monroe and Charles Laughton starred in *Full House*, a film featuring five O. Henry's short stories. The film included *The Cop and the Anthem*, *The Clarion Call*, *The Last Leaf*, *The Ransom of Red Chief*, and *The Gift of the Magi*.

O. Henry was a gifted short story writer and left us a rich legacy of great stories to enjoy.

From *The Gift of the Magi* by O. Henry

Jim drew a package from his overcoat pocket and threw it upon the table.

"Don't make any mistake, Dell," he said, "about me. I don't think there's anything in the way of a haircut or a shave or a shampoo that could make me like my girl any less. But if you'll unwrap that package you may see why you had me going a while at first."

White fingers and nimble tore at the string and paper. And then an ecstatic scream of joy; and then, alas! a quick feminine change to hysterical tears and wails, necessitating the immediate employment of all the comforting powers of the lord of the flat. For there lay The Combs – the set of combs, side and back, that Della had worshipped long in a Broadway window. Beautiful combs, pure tortoise shell, with jewelled rims

– just the shade to wear in the beautiful vanished hair. They were expensive combs, she knew, and her heart had simply craved and yearned over them without the least hope of possession. And now, they were hers, but the tresses that should have adorned the coveted adornments were gone.

But she hugged them to her bosom, and at length she was able to look up with dim eyes and a smile and say: "My hair grows so fast, Jim!"

And then Della leaped up like a little singed cat and cried, "Oh, oh!"

Jim had not yet seen his beautiful present. She held it out to him eagerly upon her open palm. The dull precious metal seemed to flash with a reflection of her bright and ardent spirit.

"Isn't it a dandy, Jim? I hunted all over town to find it. You'll have to look at the time a hundred times a day now. Give me your watch. I want to see how it looks on it."

Instead of obeying, Jim tumbled down on the couch and put his hands under the back of his head and smiled.

"Dell," said he, "let's put our Christmas presents away and keep 'em awhile. They're too nice to use just at present. I sold the watch to get the money to buy your combs. And now suppose you put the chops on."

The magi, as you know, were wise men – wonderfully wise men – who brought gifts to the Babe in the manger. They invented the art of giving Christmas presents. Being wise, their gifts were no doubt wise ones, possibly bearing the privilege of exchange in case of duplication. And here I have lamely related to you the uneventful chronicle of two foolish children in a flat who most unwisely sacrificed for each other the greatest treasures of their house. But in a last word to the wise of these days let it be said that of all who give gifts these two were the wisest. Of all who give and receive gifts, such as they are wisest.

Everywhere they are wisest. They are the magi.

Task 1. Find out what jobs did O. Henry try before becoming a writer. Compare with other writers. Task 2. Make a table of O. Henry's life and literary activity; use it to retell his biography in pairs. Task 3. In groups, name some of O. Henry's short stories having the most unexpected endings.

Task 4. Choose one of the stories and retell it to your parents to make them interested in O. Henry's works. In class, inform the others of the results – if your parents got interested to be eager to read more.

Task 5. As a group, choose a story to dramatize it for the school *Festival of American Literature*.

Task 6. What were the most precious possessions of the young couple in the story above? Read the full story and find the description of them. Write out the words making this description so vivid.

Task 7. Find out more about the magi: who were they and why are they mentioned here?

Task 8. What is a sacrifice? Brainstorm some examples of sacrifices in groups, then compare in class.

Write an essay on the topic what sacrifice is for you. What are you ready to sacrifice, and what for?

Jack London

(born John Griffith Chaney)

(January 12, 1876 – November 22, 1916)

London was a famous American novelist, short story writer, journalist, and social activist.

The future writer was born in San Francisco, California. His father was an attorney, journalist and astrologer, and his mother was a music teacher. As a baby, Jack was partially brought up by Virginia Prentiss, an African-American woman and former slave. He treasured their relationship throughout his life. But his father was never part of John's life, and his mother married John London, a Civil War veteran, who moved his new family to Oakland, where the boy studied at a public school.

Jack London called his childhood years the hungriest period of his life. He knew hard unqualified labor since the early age. As a schoolboy, when he was nine, he delivered morning and evening newspapers. Since the age of thirteen, he dived for oysters, worked on a seal-hunting ship, at a cannery, at a jute mill,

took part in the march of the unemployed to Washington to demand bread and justice, and even was a tramp (he spent a month in prison for that). In his free time, though, he visited libraries, reading novels and travel books.

In 1893, London got the \$25 first prize for a story about his sea adventures from a local newspaper.

The contest was an eye-opening experience, and he decided to dedicate his life to writing short stories.

In 1894, London began to go to Oakland High School. He desperately wanted to attend the University of California, Berkeley. In 1896, after a summer of intense studying to pass certification exams, he was admitted. However, financial circumstances forced him to leave in 1897 and he never graduated. The same year he and his sister's husband joined the Klondike Gold Rush. They headed north to Canada to seek at least a small fortune in the Yukon. The hard life conditions there undermined his health, but inspired a lot of successful stories. He began seeing writing as a business, his ticket out of poverty.

On returning to California in 1898, he had to take different odd jobs again and began working to get published, a struggle described in his novel *Martin Eden* (1909). At first, all his manuscripts were rejected. At the cost of tremendous hardships his efforts were rewarded with success: his story *To the Man on Trail* (1898) was published. Within the following four years London published his collections of northern stories – *The Son of the Wolf* (1900), *The God of his Fathers* (1901), *Children of the Frost* (1902), *A Daughter of the Snows* (1903). In 1902, working as a correspondent, the writer visited London.

In 1900, London married Bess Maddern, and the couple had two daughters. In 1905, following his divorce from Bess, London married Charmian Kittredge, with whom he was for the rest of his life. She was his soul-mate, always at his side, and they travelled a lot: about the USA, to Hawaii and Australia.

In 1904, he worked as a war correspondent in Japan, but was arrested three times by Japanese authorities, and had to return home after being released due to the interference of President Theodore Roosevelt. In 1906, he published his eye-witness report of the famous San Francisco earthquake. He shared socialist views and fought for the rights of common labourers.

A prolific writer, he published more than 50 books over the last 16 years of his life. The most famous novels are *The Call of the Wild* (1903), *The People of the Abyss* (1903), *The Sea-Wolf* (1904), *White Fang* (1906), *The South Sea Tales* (1907), *The Iron Heel* (1908), *Martin Eden* (1909), the autobiography *John Barleycorn* (1913), *The Little Lady of the Big House* (1915), *Hearts of Three* (published in 1920). The most widely known stories include *To build a Fire, All Gold Canyon, The Law of Life, Love of Life, An Odyssey of the North* (about the Klondike); *The Mexican, A Piece of Steak* (about boxing); *The Shadow and the Flash* (science fiction). There were 19 collections of short stories published during his life.

From *Martin Eden* by Jack London

...He went back to the text and lost himself. He did not notice that a young woman had entered the room. The first he knew was when he heard Arthur's voice saying: –

"Ruth, this is Mr. Eden."

The book was closed on his forefinger, and before he turned he was thrilling to the first new impression, which was not of the girl, but of her brother's words. Under that muscled body of his he was a mass of quivering sensibilities. At the slightest impact of the outside world upon his consciousness, his thoughts, sympathies, and emotions leapt and played like lambent flame. He was extraordinarily receptive and responsive, while his imagination, pitched high, was ever at work establishing relations of likeness and difference. "Mr. Eden," was what he had thrilled to – he who had been called "Eden," or "Martin Eden," or just "Martin," all his life. And "Mister!"...

And then he turned and saw the girl. The phantasmagoria of his brain vanished at sight of her. She was a pale, ethereal creature, with wide, spiritual blue eyes and a wealth of golden hair. He did not know how she was dressed, except that the dress was as wonderful as she. He likened her to a pale gold flower upon a slender stem. No, she was a spirit, a divinity, a goddess; such sublimated beauty was not of the earth. Or perhaps the books were right, and there were many such as she in the upper walks of life. ... He saw her hand coming out to his, and she looked him straight in the eyes as she shook hands, frankly, like a man. The women he had known did not shake hands that way. For that matter, most of them did not shake hands at all. A flood of associations, visions of various ways he had made the acquaintance of women, rushed into his mind and threatened to swamp it. But he shook them aside and looked at her. Never had he seen such a woman. The women he had known! Immediately, beside her, on either hand, ranged the women he had known. For an eternal second he stood in the midst of a portrait gallery, wherein she occupied the central place, while about her were limned many women, all to be weighed and measured by a fleeting glance, herself the unit of weight and measure. He saw the weak and sickly faces of the girls of the factories, and the simpering, boisterous girls from the south of Market. There were women of the cattle camps, and swarthy cigarette-smoking women of Old Mexico. These, in turn, were crowded out by Japanese women, doll-like, stepping mincingly on wooden clogs; by Eurasians, delicate featured, stamped with degeneracy; by full-bodied South-Sea-Island women, flower-crowned and brown-skinned. ...

"Won't you sit down, Mr. Eden?" the girl was saying. "I have been looking forward to meeting you ever since Arthur told us. It was brave of you – "

He waved his hand deprecatingly and muttered that it was nothing at all, what he had done, and that any fellow would have done it. She noticed that the hand he waved was covered with fresh abrasions, in the process of healing, and a glance at the other loose-hanging hand showed it to be in the same condition. Also, with quick, critical eye, she noted a scar on his cheek, another that peeped out from under the hair of the forehead, and a third that ran down and disappeared under the starched collar. She repressed a smile at sight of the red line that marked the chafe of the collar against the bronzed neck. He was evidently unused to stiff collars. ...

"You have such a scar on your neck, Mr. Eden," the girl was saying. "How did it happen? I am sure it must have been some adventure."

"A Mexican with a knife, miss," he answered, moistening his parched lips and clearing his throat. "It was just a fight. After I got the knife away, he tried to bite off my nose."

Task 1. Can we call Jack London's life "from rags to riches"? Prove your answer with the facts. Task 2. Make a table of Jack London's life and literary activity; use it to retell his biography.

Task 3. Decide in pairs what was Martin Eden's social background judging from the extract.

Task 4. What can we conclude about the destinations Martin Eden had been to in course of his life? Task 5. Choose a part from the novel *Martin Eden* to dramatize as a group for the school festival.

American literature of the first half of the 20th century

At the turn of the century, the era of social investigation began in American literature. Striking distinctions between classes became obvious: on the one hand luxurious life of businessmen, bankers and industrial tycoons, and on the other hand the working people, hardly able to make a living. Social conflicts found their reflection in different genres of literature, which was also influenced by the European writers, especially by the French school of *Naturalism* (e.g. Emile Zola).

Many writers of this period had direct experience of the World War I, and used it for their writings. They expressed the disillusionment, which followed the war. American authors wrote not only is the USA, but also in Paris and London. Experimentation in style and form was a result of the influence of contemporary art and music.

The radical economic and social changes in American life during the 1920s and 1930s marked a fruitful time for critical realists. The writers reflected the new realities of American life. New themes, plots and heroes appeared in the novels and stories of the realistic writers. Their writing became more true-to-life, thus finding understanding in their readers.

Together with the books, whose only purpose was to entertain the reader, there appeared the books containing deep analysis of the arising social problems. Realistic fiction is distinguished by a great interest in social conflicts, attacks of accepted values and criticism of the modern way of life. Among the most outstanding American realists, who revealed in their works the truth of the contemporary life, showed the tragic fate of young Americans after World War II, reflected the struggle against fascism, exposed industrial conditions and spoke out warmly in defence of labour were Dreiser, Fitzgerald, Faulkner and Hemingway.

Sinclair Lewis (the Nobel Prize 1930), Sherwood Anderson, John Dos Passos and Robert Frost also wrote about the life in America in that period of time.

American Drama

American drama as a part of literature hardly existed before 1890. Plays had been written and produced much earlier, but the stories they told had too little relation to actual life to be called literature. But after 1910 new little theatres appeared. The most famous of them was the Provincetown Players. In 1915, a group of playwrights and actors began to read and perform one-act plays on the self-made stage in Princetown. Then they went to New York and began the performances that were to shape modern American drama. Among them was the playwright **Eugene O'Neill** (1888-1953), the founder of the 20th century theatre. He constantly searched for new techniques, skilfully combining them with the old ones. O'Neill enriched his art by understanding the new psychology, the enlarged awareness of all conscious and subconscious realities. He was awarded four Pulitzer Prizes and the Nobel Prize. Due to him, American drama attained international status in the 1920s and 1930s. In the middle of the 20th century American Drama was dominated by **Tennessee Williams** and **Arthur Miller**.

Task 1. Find out general trends of the development of world literature at the turn of the 20th century. Task 2. Clarify the influence of World War I on the topics and trends of American literature.

Task 3. In pairs, discuss the problems touched upon in realistic literature of that time, and summarize them as a group. How did World War II influence the development of literature?

Task 4. In groups, exchange your knowledge about the mentioned writers and their place in literature. Task 5. Surf the Internet to learn more about the creative activity of the above-mentioned playwrights,

find out the titles of their plays; exchange your information with each other as a group.

Task 6. Find some information about modern American drama and theatre to share it in class. Make a presentation.

Theodore Herman Albert Dreiser

(August 27, 1871 – December 28, 1945)

Dreiser was a famous American novelist and journalist of the naturalist school.

Dreiser was born in the little town Terre Haute, Indiana, the second youngest child in the family of ten children. His father was a bankrupt small businessman, a strict Catholic, narrow-minded and despotic. The father's religious fanaticism, the mother's gentle tenderness, and the family's unbearable poverty worked together in shaping the young Dreiser, who was full of a furious energy, a determination to succeed, and an unalterable will. The boy dreamed of Chicago, the magic city where young men and women of the Midwest sought their fortunes. First, he had to earn his living by doing odd jobs. He worked as a waiter, a dish-washer, a rent-collector, a laundry-worker and did other low-paid temporary jobs.

His elder brother Paul became a successful song writer, and later helped Theodore establish himself in life.

After graduating from high school in Warsaw, Indiana, Dreiser attended Indiana University in 1889-1890 before dropping out because of money difficulties.

He moved from job to job until he eventually found employment with the Daily Globe, Chicago's smallest newspaper. For the next decade, he was occupied only with journalism – as a reporter and as a magazine editor – in Chicago, St. Luis, then in New York. He even happened to interview Thomas Edison.

In his first two novels, Sister Carrie (1900) and Jenny Gerhardt (1911) Dreiser described the life of two young women in the cruel society, as he himself saw it, creating a sympathetic portrait of a "sinful" woman.

It is interesting to mention that Dreiser was going to return from his first European vacation on the Titanic, but an English publisher recommended him to board a cheaper ship.

Dreiser's other works include the monumental *Trilogy of Desire*, which was based on the real life of a Chicago streetcar tycoon. It is composed of *The Financier* (1912), *The Titan* (1914), and *The Stoic* (published posthumously in 1947). The trilogy is built around the image of the businessman Frank Cowperwood and written in the tradition of literary naturalism, which was Dreiser's hallmark. *The Genius* (1915) tells about the fate of an artist in the cruel world. Though known primarily as a novelist, Dreiser also wrote short stories; his first collection, *Free and Other Stories*, appeared in 1918. *An American Tragedy* (1925) is Dreiser's masterpiece. The author emphasized the idea that not only Clyde Griffiths, the man who is convicted for the murder of his pregnant girl-friend, but society as well is held responsible for the tragedy. The society fascinated Griffiths with its glitter and wealth without providing him with a background of moral restraint.

Later on, Dreiser turned to socialism. The books *Dreiser Looks at Russia* (1928), *Tragic America* (1931) and *America Is Worth Saving* (1941) express his faith in socialist reforms. Dreiser's theories of art and philosophy of life are expressed in his nonfictional autobiographical works: *A Traveler at Forty* (1913), *A Hoosier Holiday* (1916), *A Book About Myself* (1922) (later published as *Newspaper Days*), and especially the collection of essays *Hey-Rub-a-Dub-Dub: A Book of the Mystery and Terror and Wonder of Life* (1920).

Dreiser died in Hollywood, California. Two novels were published after his death: *The Bulwark* (1946) and *The Stoic* (1947).

Task 1. How did Dreiser's young years influence his further life? Name his jobs as a young person. Task 2. Make a table of Dreiser's life and literary activity; use it to retell his biography.

Task 3. In groups, make a list of his works according to their topics; compare it with other groups.

From *An American Tragedy* by Theodore Dreiser

...Griffiths senior suddenly observed: "I had a curious experience in Chicago this time, something I think the rest of you will be interested in." He was thinking of an accidental encounter two days before in Chicago between himself and the eldest son, as it proved to be, of his younger brother Asa. Also of a conclusion he had come to in regard of him.

"Oh, what is it, Daddy?" pleaded Bella at once. "Do tell me about it."

"Spin the big news, Dad," added Gilbert, who, because of the favour of his father, felt very free and close to him always.

"Well, while I was in Chicago at the Union League Club, I met a young man who is related to us, a cousin of you three children, by the way, the eldest son of my brother Asa, who is out in Denver now, I understand. I haven't seen or heard from him in thirty years." He paused and mused dubiously.

"Not the one who is a preacher somewhere, Daddy?" inquired Bella, looking up.

"Yes, the preacher. At least I understand he was for a while after he left home. But his son tells me he has given that up now. He's connected with something in Denver – a hotel, I think."

"But what's his son like?" interrogated Bella, who only knew such well groomed and ostensibly conservative youths and men as her present social status and supervision permitted, and in consequence was intensely interested. The son of a western hotel proprietor!

"A cousin? How old is he?" asked Gilbert instantly, curious as to his character and situation and ability.

"Well, he's a very interesting young man, I think," continued Griffiths tentatively and somewhat dubiously, since up to this hour he had not truly made up his mind about Clyde. "He's quite good-looking and well-mannered, too – about your own age, I should say, Gil, and looks a lot like you – very much so – same eyes and mouth and chin." He looked at his son examiningly. "He's a little bit taller, if anything, and looks a little thinner, though I don't believe he really is."

At the thought of a cousin who looked like him – possibly as attractive in every way as himself – and bearing his own name, Gilbert chilled and bristled slightly. For here in Lycurgus, up to this time, he was well and favourably known as the only son and heir presumptive to the managerial control of his father's business, and to at least a third of the estate, if not more. And now, if by any chance it should come to light that there was a relative, a cousin of his own years and one who looked and acted like him, even – he bridled at the thought. Forthwith (a psychic reaction which he did not understand and could not very well control) he decided that he did not like him – could not like him.

"What's he doing now?" he asked in a curt and rather sour tone, though he attempted to avoid the latter element in his voice.

'Well, he hasn't much of a job, I must say," smiled Samuel Griffiths, meditatively. "He's only a bell- hop in the Union League Club in Chicago, at present, but a very pleasant and gentlemanly sort of a boy, I will say. I was quite taken with him. In fact, because he told me there wasn't much opportunity for advancement where he was, and that he would like to get into something where there was more chance to do something and be somebody, I told him if he wanted to come on here and try his luck with us, we might do a little something for him – give him a chance to show what he could do, at least."

...A cousin who was a Griffiths and good-looking and about Gilbert's age – and who, as their father reported, was rather pleasant and well-mannered – that pleased Bella and Myra while Mrs. Griffiths, noting Gilbert's face darken, was not so moved. He would not like him.

Task 1. In pairs, decide what we can infer about the family from the extract; cooperate with others. Task 2. In groups, describe each person's attitude to the news told by the father, in its development.

Task 3. Brainstorm the lexical means which make the episode clear and vivid; make use of the spotted lexis to describe a person or a situation to your liking.

F. Scott Fitzgerald

(born Francis Scott Key Fitzgerald)

(September 24, 1896 – December 21, 1940)

Fitzgerald was a famous American short-story writer and novelist.

Born in St. Paul, Minnesota, to an upper-middle-class family, he was named after his famous second cousin on his father's side, Francis Scott Key, who wrote the lyrics to the *Star-Spangled Banner*, the national anthem of the USA. The boy spent his childhood in Buffalo, New York, and in West Virginia. Fitzgerald was a bright, handsome and ambitious boy, the pride and joy of his parents and especially his mother. He attended the St. Paul Academy, and when he was 13, his first story was published in the school newspaper. At the age of 15, he was sent to the Newman School, a prestigious Catholic preparatory school in New Jersey, and after graduating from it in 1913, entered Princeton University. There he wrote scripts for musicals, articles for a humor

magazine, and stories. In 1917, he dropped out before graduating to join the U.S. Army. Within some weeks Fitzgerald hastily wrote a novel *The Romantic Egotist*, but it was rejected by a publisher.

It was in the army in Alabama that he met and fell in love with a beautiful 18-year-old girl named Zelda Sayre. When the war ended in November 1918, he moved to New York City and worked briefly for an advertising agency. Then he returned to St. Paul to rewrite his novel.

The novel's new incarnation, *This Side of Paradise* was published in 1920 and, almost overnight, turned Fitzgerald, at the age of 24, into one of the country's most promising young writers. One week after the novel's publication, he married the woman he loved, his muse Zelda in New York, and they had a daughter. The family lived in Great Neck, New York.

Following his literary success, F. Scott Fitzgerald started an extravagant lifestyle that earned him a reputation of a playboy; he also took to drinking. Nevertheless, he continued writing. In 1922, Fitzgerald published his second novel, *The Beautiful and Damned*.

In 1924, Fitzgerald moved to France, and there he wrote his greatest novel, *The Great Gatsby* (1925). The story is narrated by Nick Carraway, a Midwesterner who moves into the town of West Egg on Long Island, next door to a mansion owned by the wealthy and mysterious Jay Gatsby. The novel follows Nick and Gatsby's strange friendship and Gatsby's love to a married woman named Daisy, ultimately leading to his death. With its beautiful lyricism, perfect portrayal of the Jazz Age, love and the American Dream, *The Great Gatsby* is considered Fitzgerald's finest work and one of the greatest American novels ever written.

In the following years, the Fitzgeralds travelled back and forth between Europe and the States several times. For a while, he worked in Hollywood as a screenwriter. Unfortunately, he had problems with alcohol; his wife had a mental breakdown in 1930, and was treated at mental health clinics for years.

The fourth novel, *Tender is the Night* appeared in 1934, but it was not a success.

In 1937 Fitzgerald attempted to revive his career as a screenwriter in Hollywod. He died of a heart attack in Hollywood, California, his final novel *The Love of the Last Tycoon*, only half completed.

Apart from his five novels, Fitzgerald was the author of 4 collections of short stories and 164 short stories in magazines. Some of his most notable stories are *The Diamond as Big as the Ritz, The Curious Case of Benjamin Button, The Camel's Back* and *The Last of the Belles.*

Though he received limited success in his lifetime, F. Scott Fitzgerald is now widely regarded as one of the greatest American writers of the 20th century.

Task 1. Listen to the American national anthem, then find its lyrics and work on it in groups. Task 2. Make a table of Fitzgerald's life and literary activity; use it to retell his biography.

Task 3. Learn more about Fitzgerald's work as a screenwriter in Hollywood; deliver it in class.

From *The Great Gatsby* by F. Scott Fitzgerald

I was still with Jordan Baker. We were sitting at a table with a man of about my age and a rowdy little girl who gave way upon the slightest provocation to uncontrollable laughter. I was enjoying myself now. I had taken two finger bowls of champagne and the scene had changed before my eyes into something significant, elemental and profound.

At a lull in the entertainment the man looked at me and smiled.

"Your face is familiar," he said, politely. "Weren't you in the Third Division during the war?" "Why, yes. I was in the Ninth Machine-Gun Battalion."

"I was in the Seventh Infantry until June nineteen-eighteen. I knew I'd seen you somewhere before."

We talked for a moment about some wet, grey little villages in France. Evidently he lived in this vicinity for he told me that he had just bought a hydroplane and was going to try it out in the morning.

"Want to go with me, old sport? Just near the shore along the Sound." "What time?"

"Any time that suits you best."

It was on the tip of my tongue to ask his name when Jordan looked around and smiled. "Having a gay time now?" she inquired.

"Much better." I turned again to my new acquaintance. "This is an unusual party for me. I haven't even seen the host. I live over there –" I waved my hand at the invisible hedge in the distance, "and this man Gatsby sent over his chauffeur with an invitation."

For a moment he looked at me as if he failed to understand. "I'm Gatsby," he said suddenly.

"What!" I exclaimed. "Oh, I beg your pardon."

"I thought you knew, old sport. I'm afraid I'm not a very good host."

He smiled understandingly – much more than understandingly. It was one of those rare smiles with a quality of eternal reassurance in it, that you may come across four or five times in life. It faced – or seemed to face – the whole external world for an instant, and then concentrated on YOU with an irresistible prejudice in your favour. It understood you just so far as you wanted to be understood, believed in you as you would like to believe in yourself and assured you that it had precisely the impression of you that, at your best, you hoped to convey.

Precisely at that point it vanished – and I was looking at an elegant young rough- neck, a year or two over thirty, whose elaborate formality of speech just missed being absurd. Some time before he introduced himself I'd got a strong impression that he was picking his words with care.

Almost at the moment when Mr. Gatsby identified himself a butler hurried toward him with the information that Chicago was calling him on the wire. He excused himself with a small bow that included each of us in turn.

"If you want anything just ask for it, old sport," he urged me. "Excuse me. I will rejoin you later."

When he was gone I turned immediately to Jordan – constrained to assure her of my surprise. I had expected that Mr. Gatsby would be a florid and corpulent person in his middle years.

"Who is he?" I demanded. "Do you know?" "He's just a man named Gatsby."

"Where is he from, I mean? And what does he do?"

..."Well, he told me once he was an Oxford man."

A dim background started to take shape behind him but at her next remark it faded away. "However, I don't believe it."

Task 1. In pairs, decide what we learn about the characters of the book from the extract. Task 2. In groups, explore the literary means used to describe the host's smile, and their role.

Task 3. Get acquainted with the content of the novel and retell it in class to the other students.

William Faulkner

(born William Cuthbert Falkner)

(September 25, 1897 – July 6, 1962)

Faulkner was an outstanding novelist of the American South, who got the Nobel Prize (1949), two Pulitzer prizes, two National Book Awards, and the Legion of Honor in New Orleans.

Faulkner was born in New Albany, Mississippi, the first of four sons in an impoverished aristocratic family. He was named after his great-grandfather, William Clark Falkner, a successful businessman, writer and Civil War hero. When the future writer was five, the family settled in Oxford, Mississippi, and he spent the rest of his life mostly there. His father worked as the business

manager for the University of Mississippi. Faulkner's nanny was a black woman. She raised him from birth until the day he left home and crucially influenced his development.

As a teenager, Faulkner enjoyed drawing, reading and writing poetry. He was fascinated by Scottish romantics, especially Robert Burns. However, despite his remarkable intelligence, or, perhaps, because of it, school bored him and he never earned a high school diploma. After dropping out in 1914, Faulkner worked in carpentry and as a clerk at his grandfather's bank.

During this time, Faulkner fell in love with Estelle Oldham. However, she married another man. He finally managed to marry her only in 1929, when she got divorced; they had a daughter. The publishing of several stories brought Faulkner enough money to buy a house in Oxford for his family in 1930.

In 1917, he moved to New Haven, Connecticut, began writing and worked at a rifle manufacturing factory. The war being in progress in Europe, he joined the British Royal Flying Corps in 1918 and trained as a pilot in the Canadian Air Force. He had earlier tried to enlist in the U.S. Forces, but was rejected due to his small height. To enlist in the Royal Air Force, he lied about several facts, changing his birthplace and surname – from Falkner to Faulkner – to appear more British. Faulkner trained on British and Canadian bases, and finished his training in Toronto just before the war ended – so, he did not take part in it.

In 1919, Faulkner enrolled at the University of Mississippi in

Oxford. However, after three semesters as an entirely imprudent student, he dropped out. He worked briefly in New York City as a bookseller's assistant, and for two years as the postmaster for the university, and as a scoutmaster.

His volume of poems *The Marble Faun* was published in 1924, but it was not successful. Faulkner moved to New Orleans, Louisiana. While there, he published several essays. In 1926, Faulkner succeeded in having his first novel published, *Soldiers' Pay*. As soon as it had been accepted for print in 1925, he sailed from New Orleans to Europe to live for a few months in Paris.

Faulkner began writing about the places and people of his childhood, developing a great many colorful characters based on real people, including his great-grandfather, William Clark Falkner. He wrote the novels *Mosquitos* (1927), *Sartoris* (1928). For his famous novel, *The Sound and the Fury* (1929), he developed the fictional Yoknapatawpha County – a place nearly identical to Lafayette County, in which Oxford, Mississippi, is located. Faulkner's next novels were *As I Lay Dying* (1930), *Sanctuary* (1931), *Light in August* (1932), *Absalom, Absalom!* (1936), *The Hamlet* (1940), *Go Down, Moses* (1942), *Intruder in the Dust* (1948), *Requiem for a Nun* (1950), *The Fable* (1954), *The Town* (1957), *The Reivers* (1962).

After publishing several notable books, Faulkner turned to screenwriting. Between 1932 and 1945, he traveled to Hollywood a dozen times. Uninspired by the job, however, he did it purely for financial gain.

Faulkner died of a heart attack as a result of a horse-riding accident.

He created an impressive literary legacy. Some of his books were made into films.

Task 1. Make a chronological table of Faulkner's life and creative activity and discuss it in pairs. Task 2. Choose a period of Faulkner's life you are interested in and learn more about it.

From *The Sound and the Fury* by William Faulkner

The church had been decorated, with sparse flowers from kitchen gardens and hedgerows, and with streamers of coloured crepe paper. Above the pulpit hung a battered Christmas bell, the accordian sort that collapses. The pulpit was empty, though the choir was already in place, fanning themselves although it was not warm.

Most of the women were gathered on one side of the room. They were talking. Then the bell struck one time and they dispersed to their seats and the congregation sat for an instant, expectant. The bell struck again one time. The choir rose and began to sing and the congregation turned its head as one, as six small children – four girls with tight pigtails bound with small scraps of cloth like butterflies, and two boys with close napped heads, – entered and marched up the aisle, strung together in a harness of white ribbons and flowers, and followed by two men in single file. The second man was huge, of a light coffee colour, imposing in a frock coat and white tie. His head was magisterial and profound, his neck rolled above his collar in rich folds. But he was familiar to them, and so the heads were still reverted when he had passed, and it was not until the choir ceased singing that they realised that the visiting clergyman had already entered, and when they saw the man who had preceded their minister enter the pulpit still ahead of him an indescribable sound went up, a sigh, a sound of astonishment and disappointment.

The visitor was undersized, in a shabby alpaca coat. He had a wizened black face like a small, aged monkey. And all the while that the choir sang again and while the six children rose and sang in thin, frightened, tuneless whispers, they watched the insignificant looking man sitting dwarfed and countrified by the minister's imposing bulk, with something like consternation. They were still looking at him with consternation and unbelief when the minister rose and introduced him in rich, rolling tones whose very unction served to increase the visitor's insignificance...

When the visitor rose to speak he sounded like a white man. His voice was level and cold. It sounded too big to have come from him and they listened at first through curiosity, as they would have to a monkey talking. They began to watch him as they would a man on a tight rope. They even forgot his insignificant appearance in the virtuosity with which he ran and poised and swooped upon the cold inflectionless wire of his voice, so that at last, when with a sort of swooping glide he came to rest again beside the reading desk with one arm resting upon it at shoulder height and his monkey body as reft of all motion as a mummy or an emptied vessel, the congregation sighed as if waked from a collective dream and moved a little in its seats. Behind the pulpit the choir fanned steadily. Dilsey whispered, "Hush, now. They are fixing to sing in a minute."

Then a voice said, "Brethren."

The preacher had not moved. His arm lay yet across the desk, and he still held that pose while the voice died in sonorous echoes between the walls. It was as different as day and dark from his former tone, with a sad, timbrous quality like an alto horn, sinking into their hearts and speaking there again when it had ceased in fading and cumulate echoes.

"Brethren   and   sisteren,"   it   said   again...

Task 1. Write out the words in which the church is described. In pairs, track down their formation and

Task 2. In groups, identify the words describing the children; exchange your lists with other groups. Task 3. Individually, distribute the words describing the stranger according to the parts of speech;
compare the results as a group; then use some of them in the sentences of your own.
Task 4. Get acquainted with the content of the novel and write a critical essay about it.

Ernest Miller Hemingway
(July 21, 1899 – July 2, 1961)

Hemingway was a great American novelist, short story writer and journalist, the author of ten novels, ten short story collections and five non-fiction works. He was awarded the Nobel Prize (1954) and the Pulitzer Prize (1953).

Hemingway was born in Cicero (now Oak Park), a suburb of Chicago, Illinois, second of five children. His father was a physician, and his mother was a musician. In high school, Hemingway worked on his school newspaper and was an excellent sportsman. Immediately after graduation, at 17, he went to work for *The Kansas City Star*. In 1918, Hemingway went overseas to serve in World War I as an ambulance driver in the Italian Army. For his service, he was awarded the Italian Silver Medal of Bravery. He was wounded and taken to a hospital in Milan. There he met a nurse named Agnes von Kurowsky, who soon accepted his proposal of marriage, but later left him for another man. This devastated the young writer but provided the basis for some of his works.

At the age of 20, he returned to the United States and spent time in northern Michigan before taking a job at the *Toronto Star*. In Chicago Hemingway met Hadley Richardson, his first wife. The couple married in 1921 and soon moved to Paris, where Hemingway worked as a foreign correspondent for the *Star*. At this period he was described as a "tall, handsome, muscular, broad-shouldered, brown-eyed, rosy-cheeked, square-jawed, soft-voiced young man." The couple had a son.

In Paris, Hemingway joined "The Lost Generation" expatriate community and made the acquaintance of many great writers and artists of his generation, such as F. Scott Fitzgerald, Ezra Pound, Pablo Picasso and James Joyce. He described this experience in his first novel, *The Sun Also Rises* (1926).

In 1927, the journalist Pauline Pfeiffer became his second wife, and they had two sons. Hemingway worked on his book of short stories, *Men Without Women* (1927). Soon the couple moved back to America and settled in Key West, Florida, but summered in Wyoming. At this time, Hemingway finished his celebrated novel about World War I *A Farewell to Arms* (1929) about an American ambulance officer.

While reporting on the Spanish Civil War in 1937, Hemingway gathered material for his book of short stories *The Fifth Column and the First Forty-Nine Stories* (1938) and his next novel, *For Whom the Bell Tolls* (1940). He met a war correspondent Martha Gellhorn, who became his third wife in 1940, and they soon purchased a farm near Havana, Cuba, where their winter residence was; he kept there dozens of cats.

When the United States entered World War II in 1941, Hemingway served as a correspondent and was present at some key moments of the war, including the Normandy landings and the liberation of Paris. At the end of the war, Hemingway met another war correspondent, Mary Welsh, whom he married in 1946. In 1947, he was awarded a Bronze Star for his bravery during World War II.

In 1951, Hemingway wrote his outstanding short novel *The Old Man and the Sea*, the story of Santiago, an old Cuban fisherman, his long and lonely struggle with a giant fish and the sea far out in the Gulf Stream off the coast of Florida, and his victory in defeat. It made him an international celebrity.

During all his life, Hemingway spent much of his time chasing adventure: big-game safari hunting in Africa, bullfighting in Spain, deep-sea fishing in Florida, sailing in the Caribbean. He had several serious injuries, even surviving some plane crashes; he also drank a lot. At the end of his life he suffered from depression and diseases. He bought a house in Ketchum, Idaho, where he committed suicide.

Hemingway left an impressive literary legacy. His principles were: to be honest and to write the absolute truth, to write only when you can't help it, and to write about what you know very well. He portrayed soldiers, hunters, bullfighters – tough, sometimes primitive people, whose courage and honesty are set against the brutal ways of modern society, and who in this confrontation at times lose hope and faith.

From *The Old Man and the Sea* by Ernest Hemingway

...Everything about him was old except his eyes and they were the same color as the sea and were cheerful and undefeated.

"Santiago," the boy said to him as they climbed the bank from where the skiff was hauled up. "I could go with you again. We've made some money."

The old man had taught the boy to fish and the boy loved him. "No," the old man said. "You're with a lucky boat. Stay with them."

"But remember how you went eighty-seven days without fish and then we caught big ones every day for three weeks."

"I remember," the old man said. "I know you did not leave me because you doubted." "It was papa made me leave. I am a boy and I must obey him."

"I know,' the old man said. "It is quite normal." "He hasn't much faith."

"No," the old man said. "But we have. Haven't we?"

"Yes," the boy said. "Can I offer you a beer on the Terrace and then we'll take the stuff home." "Why not?" the old man said. "Between fishermen."

They sat on the Terrace and many of the fishermen made fun of the old man and he was not angry. Others, of the older fishermen, looked at him and were sad. But they did not show it and they spoke politely about the current and the depths they had drifted their lines at and the steady good weather and of what they had seen. The successful fishermen of that day were already in and had butchered their marlin out and carried them laid full length across two planks, with two men staggering at the end of each plank, to the fish house where they waited for the ice truck to carry them to the market in Havana. Those who had caught sharks had taken them to the shark factory on the other side of the cove where they were hoisted on a block and tackle, their livers removed, their fins cut off and their hides skinned out and their flesh cut into strips for salting.

When the wind was in the east a smell came across the harbour from the shark factory; but today there was only the faint edge of the odour because the wind had backed into the north and then dropped off and it was pleasant and sunny on the Terrace.

"Santiago," the boy said.

"Yes," the old man said. He was holding his glass and thinking of many years ago. "Can I go out to get sardines for you tomorrow?"

"No. Go and play baseball. I can still row and Rogelio will throw the net."

"I would like to go. If I cannot fish with you, I would like to serve in some way." "You bought me a beer," the old man said. "You are already a man."

"How old was I when you first took me in a boat?"

"Five and you nearly were killed when I brought the fish in too green and he nearly tore the boat to pieces. Can you remember?"

..."I remember everything from when we first went together."

The old man looked at him with his sun-burned, confident loving eyes.

"If you were my boy I'd take you out and gamble," he said. "But you are your father's and your mother's and you are in a lucky boat."

"May I get the sardines? I know where I can get four baits too." "I have mine left from today. I put them in salt in the box." "Let me get four fresh ones."

Task 1. Find out about Hemingway's war experience to share your information in class.

Task 2. Make a chronological table of Hemingway's works and exchange the results in groups. Task 3. What can we conclude from the dialogue between the fisherman and the boy in the extract?

Task 4. Get acquainted with the original text of the novel and exchange your opinions in class. Write an essay about your attitude to the main hero.

Depression era writers included **John Steinbeck** (1902-1968) (the Nobel Prize 1962), notable for his novel *The Grapes of Wrath*, and **Henry Miller**, whose works were considered controversial and were even banned in the USA for some time. Their works had a major influence on the succeeding generations of American writers.

America's involvement in World War II influenced the creative activity of the writers: Norman Mailer, Joseph Heller, Kurt Vonnegut. Harper Lee, Jerome David Salinger, William Gaddis created their works in this period, too. In African-American literature Ralph Ellison's novel *Invisible Man* (1952) was recognized as one of the most powerful and important works of the post-war years.

Among short story writers there were Flannery O'Connor, Katherine Anne Porter, Tobias Wolff.

Thomas Stearns Eliot (1888-1965) was a British essayist, playwright and poet of the American origin. He moved to England in 1914, settled, worked and married there, and took British citizenship in 1927. He got the Nobel Prize (1948) and the Order of Merit (1948). His most notable works are the poems *The Love Song of J. Alfred Prufrock* (1915), *The Waste Land* (1922), *The Hollow Men* (1925), *Ash Wednesday* (1930), *Four Quarters* (1943), and plays *Murder in the Cathedral* (1935), *The Cocktail Party* (1949). Born in St. Luis, Missouri, the last of six children in a prosperous family, he earned his bachelor's degree at Harvard College in three years instead of four. Then Eliot moved to Paris, where he studied philosophy at the Sorbonne. Back at Harvard he studied Indian philosophy and Sanskrit. In 1914, he went to Oxford but preferred to spend his time in London. He worked as a teacher at schools and at Universities of London and Oxford, and as an editor at a publishing house. He died in London, and in Poets' Corner of Westminster Abbey there is a stone in his honour.

Nelle Harper Lee (1926-2016) was a novelist best known for her Pulitzer Prize-winning bestseller *To Kill a Mockingbird* (1960). It reflects racial prejudices of the South. The attorney, Atticus Finch (who is said to have been based on Lee's father), tries to help a black man who has been charged with raping a white woman to get a fair trial and to prevent him from being lynched by angry whites. In 1962, the movie version of the book won three Academy Awards. In November 2007, President George W. Bush presented Lee with the Presidential Medal of

Freedom for her contribution to literature at a ceremony at the White House. She is also known for assisting her close friend Truman Capote in his research for the nonfiction masterpiece *In Cold Blood* (1966). Lee spent almost all her life in Monroeville, Alabama. She studied at the all-female Huntingdon College in Montgomery, then at the University of Alabama. She went to Oxford University in England as an exchange student. Lee generally lived a quiet, private life, splitting her time between New York City and her hometown of Monroeville. She was known to donate money to charity organizations.

Task 1. Find out information about one of the writers mentioned in the first part of the article, and prepare a presentation to demonstrate in class.

Task 2. Find out more about Eliot's places of living and his citizenship to inform your classmates. Task 3. Make a table of Harper Lee's life and work to exchange your information in groups.

Task 4. Get acquainted with the novel *To Kill a Mockingbird* and retell its content in class.

Margaret Munnerlyn Mitchell
(November 8, 1900 – August 16, 1949)

Mitchell was born in Atlanta, Georgia, into a wealthy family. Her father was an attorney, and her mother was a suffragist. She had an elder brother. At an early age, she loved to make up stories, and later she wrote her own adventure books, making their covers out of cardboard. She wrote hundreds of books as a child, but her literary endeavors weren't limited to stories: at the private Woodberry School, Mitchell directed and acted in plays she wrote.

In 1918, Mitchell graduated from Washington Seminary and began to study medicine at Smith College in Northampton, Massachusetts. Four months later her mother died of influenza. Mitchell finished her freshman year and returned to Atlanta to prepare for the upcoming debutante season, during which she met

Berrien Kinnard Upshaw. The couple got married in 1922, but soon divorced because of Upshaw's violent character and rude behavior.

In the same year Mitchell got a job with the *Atlanta Journal Sunday Magazine*, for which she wrote nearly 130 articles on a wide range of topics, from fashions to politics, as well as news stories and book reviews, under the name Peggy Mitchell. In 1925, she married John Robert Marsh, who was the best man at her first wedding. He was an advertising manager and encouraged her in her writing aspirations. Unfortunately, her journalist career ended in 1926 due to complications from a broken ankle, and she chose to become a full-time wife. However, having to stay in bed due to this accident, she began writing *Gone With the Wind*. She wrote the last chapter first and the other chapters randomly, and finished most of the book by 1929. A romantic novel about the Civil War and Reconstruction, *Gone with the Wind* is told from a Southern point of view.

In July 1935, the New York Publishing Company Macmillan offered her a $500 advance and 10 percent royalty payments for her book. Mitchell set to completing the manuscript, changing characters names (Scarlett was Pansy in earlier drafts), cutting and rearranging chapters and finally naming the book *Gone with the Wind*, a phrase from *"Cynara!"*, her favorite poem by the English writer of the Decadent movement Ernest Dowson. The novel was published in 1936 to huge success and took the National Book Award and the Pulitzer Prize in 1937. Mitchell became an overnight celebrity. The landmark film based on her novel came out just three years later and went on to become a classic, winning eight Oscars and two special Oscars.

During World War II, Mitchell had no time to write, as she worked for the American Red Cross, sewing hospital gowns, putting patches on trousers and writing encouraging letters to soldiers and sailors.

In 1949, she was struck by a speeding car while crossing a street and died five days later. *Gone with the Wind* was her only novel. More than 30 million copies of Mitchell's masterpiece have been sold worldwide, and it has been translated into 27 languages.

Task 1. In groups, make a chronological table of Mitchell's life to help you tell her biography. Task 2. Find out additional information about the writing of the novel to exchange in pairs.

Task 3. Find information about the film based on Mitchell's book to present at the lesson.

Task 4. In groups, analyse the description of Scarlett's appearance; choose the corresponding words. Task 5. Individually, write out the words describing her dress; compare your list in pairs.

Task 6. Brainstorm the literary means used to describe the boys, and their role in the text.

Task 7. How is the kinship between the boys and their animals described?

Task 8. As a group, decide what is peculiar about the date of the described event.

From *Gone with the Wind* by Margaret Mitchell

Scarlett O'Hara was not beautiful, but men seldom realized it when caught by her charm as the Tarleton twins were. In her face were too sharply blended the delicate features of her mother, a Coast aristocrat of French descent, and the heavy ones of her florid Irish father. But it was an arresting face, pointed of chin, square of jaw. Her eyes were pale green without a touch of hazel, starred with bristly black lashes and slightly tilted at the ends. Above them, her thick black brows slanted upward, cutting a startling oblique line in her magnolia-white skin – that skin so prized by Southern women and so carefully guarded with bonnets, veils and mittens against hot Georgia suns.

Seated with Stuart and Brent Tarleton in the cool shade of the porch of Tara, her father's plantation, that bright April afternoon of 1861, she made a pretty picture. Her new green flowered-muslin dress spread its twelve yards of billowing material over her hoops and exactly matched the flat-heeled green morocco slippers her father had recently brought her from Atlanta. The dress set off to perfection the seventeen-inch waist, the smallest in three counties, and the tightly fitted basque showed breasts well matured for her sixteen years. But for all the modesty of her spreading skirts, the demureness of hair netted smoothly into a chignon and the quietness of small white hands folded in her lap, her true self was poorly concealed. The green eyes in the carefully sweet face were turbulent, willful, lusty with life, distinctly at variance with her decorous demeanor. Her manners had been imposed upon her by her mother's gentle admonitions and the sterner discipline of her mammy; her eyes were her own.

On either side of her, the twins lounged easily in their chairs, squinting at the sunlight through tall mint-garnished glasses as they laughed and talked, their long legs, booted to the knee and thick with saddle muscles, crossed negligently. Nineteen years old, six feet two inches tall, long of bone and hard of muscle, with sunburned faces and deep auburn hair, their eyes merry and arrogant, their bodies clothed in identical blue coats and mustard-colored breeches, they were as much alike as two bolls of cotton.

Outside, the late afternoon sun slanted down in the yard, throwing into gleaming brightness the dogwood trees that were solid masses of white blossoms against the background of new green. The twins' horses were hitched in the driveway, big animals, red as their masters' hair; and around the horses' legs quarreled the pack of lean, nervous possum hounds that accompanied Stuart and Brent wherever they went. A little aloof, as became an aristocrat, lay a black-spotted carriage dog, muzzle on paws, patiently waiting for the boys to go home to supper.

Between the hounds and the horses and the twins there was a kinship deeper than that of their constant companionship. They were all healthy, thoughtless young animals, sleek, graceful, high-spirited, the boys as mettlesome as the horses they rode, mettlesome and dangerous but, withal, sweet-tempered to those who knew how to handle them.

Although born to the ease of plantation life, waited on hand and foot since infancy, the faces of the three on the porch were neither slack nor soft. They had the vigor and alertness of country people who have spent all their lives in the open and troubled their heads very little with dull things in books... The more sedate and older sections of the South looked down their noses at the up-country Georgians, but here in north Georgia, a lack of the niceties of classical education carried no shame, provided a man was smart in the things that mattered. And raising good cotton, riding well, shooting straight, dancing lightly, squiring the ladies with elegance were the things that mattered.

In these accomplishments the twins excelled, and they were equally outstanding in their notorious inability to learn anything contained between the covers of books. Their family had more money, more horses, more slaves than any one else in the County, but the boys had less grammar than most of their poor neighbors.

It was for this precise reason that Stuart and Brent were idling on the porch of Tara this April afternoon. They had just been expelled from the University of Georgia, the fourth university that had thrown them out in two years...

Jerome David Salinger

(January 1, 1919 – January 27, 2010)

Salinger was an American novelist and short story writer.

Salinger was born and grew up in the fashionable apartment district of Manhattan, Park Avenue, in New York, New York. He and his elder sister were the two children of a well-to-do Jewish businessman and his Scottish-born wife.

Despite his apparent intellect, Salinger wasn't a good student. He attended a school in New York, and then Valley Forge Military Academy in Wayne, Pennsylvania in 1934-1936. Then he  studied for a year at New York University, and in 1937 went off to Europe, to learn about the meat-importing business. He worked for five months at a company in Austria (Vienna) and Poland.

Upon returning home, he made another attempt at college, this time at Ursinus College in Pennsylvania, before coming back to New York and taking night classes at Columbia University. There,

Salinger met Professor Whit Burnett, who wasn't just a good

teacher, but also the editor of *Story* magazine, where Salinger published his first story in 1940. His works began to appear in other big-name periodicals such as *Collier's* and the *Saturday Evening Post*.

In late 1941, Salinger briefly worked on a Caribbean cruise ship as an activity director. In 1942, he started dating Oona O'Neill, daughter of the playwright Eugene O'Neill. He wrote her long letters almost daily, and was shocked when she married Charles Chaplin, who was much older than she.

World War II interrupted his career. Following the attack on Pearl Harbor, Salinger was drafted into the army, serving in infantry from 1942 till 1944. He took part in the Normandy Invasion and some other military actions. During this time, however, Salinger continued to write. In Paris he arranged to meet Ernest Hemingway, and they were corresponding for some time.

Salinger was assigned to a counter-intelligence division, for which he used his proficiency in French and German to interrogate prisoners of war. In April 1945, he entered the liberated concentration camp Dachau. It is not surprising that his war experiences affected him emotionally. He was hospitalized for a few weeks for combat stress reaction after the war. In 1946, he married a German doctor, Sylvia, and brought her to the US, but their union was just eight months long. He married Claire Douglas in 1955 and they had two children. They divorced in 1967, as he retreated into his private world and Zen Buddhism.

When Salinger returned to New York in 1946, he resumed his writing career and began publishing his works in his favorite magazine, *The New Yorker*. He also continued to work on his novel. Finally, in 1951, *The Catcher in the Rye* was published. It described a deeply unsatisfied rebellious teenage schoolboy named Holden Caulfield and his experiences in New York. The book won huge international acclaim. It was criticized for the coarse language and even banned in some schools. It remains widely read and it is still considered quite controversial. Salinger rejected numerous offers to adapt the book for the screen.

In 1953, Salinger moved from New York City to Cornish, New Hampshire and led a very private life for more than half a century. There, Salinger did his best to cut-off contact with the public and significantly slowed his literary output. He published a short story collection, Nine Stories (1953), then *Franny and Zooey* (1961); his last published work was the novella *Hapworth 16, 1924*. Afterward, Salinger struggled with undesirable attention, defending his privacy.

In 1972, Salinger met a college freshman Joyce Maynard, and they lived together in Cornish for 10 months. In 1998 Maynard wrote a negative account of her life with the writer, disclosing his evil features. A year later she auctioned off a series of letters Salinger had written her while they were still together. The letters cost $156,500. The buyer, a computer programmer, later returned them to Salinger as a gift.

In 1988, he married a young nurse named Colleen O'Neill. They were married until his death.

Salinger is considered a literary giant despite his little legacy and secluded lifestyle, due to his landmark novel *The Catcher in the Rye*.

Task 1. Make a table of Salinger's life and work to exchange your information in groups. Task 2. Learn more about any period of the writer's life to share this information in class. Task 3. Individually, find the words which explain the title of the book. What do they mean? Task 4. Work in pairs. What rude and unnecessary words can you notice in Holden's speech?

Task 5. At home, find and read the mentioned poem by Robert Burns. Do you know his other works?

From *The Catcher in the Rye* by David Salinger

Old Phoebe said something then, but I couldn't hear her. She had the side of her mouth right smack on the pillow, and I couldn't hear her.

"What?" I said. "Take your mouth away. I can't hear you with your mouth that way." "You don't like anything that's happening."

It made me even more depressed when she said that.

"Yes I do. Yes I do. Sure I do. Don't say that. Why the hell do you say that?"

"Because you don't. You don't like any schools. You don't like a million things. You don't."

"I do! That's where you're wrong – that's exactly where you're wrong! Why the hell do you have to say that?" I said. Boy, was she depressing me.

"Because you don't," she said. "Name one thing." "One thing? One thing I like?" I said. "Okay."

The trouble was, I couldn't concentrate too hot. Sometimes it's hard to concentrate... "I like Allie," I said. "And I like doing what I'm doing right now."

"Allie's dead – You always say that! If somebody's dead, and in Heaven, then it isn't really –"

"I know he's dead! Don't you think I know that? I can still like him, though, can't I? Just because somebody's dead, you don't just stop liking them, for God's sake—especially if they were about a thousand times nicer than the people you know that're alive and all."

Old Phoebe didn't say anything. When she can't think of anything to say, she doesn't say a goddam word.

"Anyway, I like it now," I said. "I mean right now. Sitting here with you, and talking, and thinking about stuff, and –"

"That isn't anything really!"

"It is so something really! Certainly it is! Why the hell isn't it? People never think anything is anything really. I'm getting goddam sick of it."

"Stop swearing. All right, name something else. Name something you'd like to be. Like a scientist. Or a lawyer or something."

"I couldn't be a scientist. I'm no good in science." "Well, a lawyer – like Daddy and all."

"Lawyers are all right, I guess—but it doesn't appeal to me," I said. "I mean they're all right if they go around saving innocent guys' lives all the time, and like that, but you don't do that kind of stuff if you're a lawyer. All you do is make a lot of dough and play golf and play bridge and buy cars and drink Martinis and look like a hot-shot. And besides. Even if you did go around saving guys' lives and all, how would you know if you did it because you really wanted to save guys' lives, or because you did it because what you really wanted to do was be a terrific lawyer, with everybody slapping you on the back and congratulating you in court when the goddam trial was over, the reporters and everybody, the way it is in the dirty movies? How would you know you weren't being a phony? The trouble is, you wouldn't."

I'm not too sure old Phoebe knew what the hell I was talking about. I mean she's only a little child and all. But she was listening, at least. If somebody at least listens, it's not too bad.

"Daddy's going to kill you. He's going to kill you," she said.

I wasn't listening, though. I was thinking about something else – something crazy. "You know what I'd like to be?" I said. "You know what I'd like to be? I mean if I had my goddam choice?"

"What? Stop swearing."

"You know that song 'If a body catch a body comin' through the rye'? I'd like –"

"It's 'If a body meet a body coming through the rye'!" old Phoebe said. "It's a poem. By Robert Burns."

"I know it's a poem by Robert Burns... Anyway, I keep picturing all these little kids playing some game in this big field of rye and all. Thousands of little kids, and nobody's around – nobody big, I mean – except me. And I'm standing on the edge of some crazy cliff. What I have to do, I have to catch everybody if they start to go over the cliff – I mean if they're running and they don't look where they're going I have to come out from somewhere and catch them. That's all I'd do all day. I'd just be the catcher in the rye and all. I know it's crazy, but that's the only thing I'd really like to be. I know it's crazy."

Old Phoebe didn't say anything for a long time.

Then, when she said something, all she said was, "Daddy's going to kill you."

<h1 style="text-align:right">Postmodernism</h1>
<h2 style="text-align:center">(early 1970s – to the present day)</h2>

Apart from modernist features, such as temporal distortion, unreliable narrators, and internal monologue, postmodern techniques include metafiction, unrealistic names, absurdist plots, hyperbolic humour, deliberate use of anachronisms and archaisms, digression, elaborate symbolism. The representatives of this trend in American literature are Toni Morrison (the Nobel Prize in 1993), Cormac McCarthy, Don DeLillo, Philip Roth, Thomas Pynchon, David Foster Wallace, Jonathan Franzen.

John Updike (1932-2009) was a novelist, poet, short story writer, who got the Pulitzer Prize for fiction twice. He majored in English at Harvard and even studied for a year in Oxford, England. The most famous is his *Rabbit* series (the novels *Rabbit, Run*; *Rabbit Redux*; *Rabbit Is Rich*; *Rabbit at Rest*; *Rabbit Remembered*) about the life of the middle-class man over the course of several decades, from young adulthood to death. Updike developed his unique prose style and wrote about the concerns, passions and suffering of average Americans. He produced about twenty novels, a dozen short story collections, children's books and poetry.

Ken Kesey (1935-2001) was a novelist, short story writer, poet and essayist. He wrote in the genre of postmodernism, and belonged to countercultural literary movement. His most notable work is the novel *One Flew Over the Cuckoo's Nest* (1962), which was an immediate success. However, he regarded the novel *Sometimes a Great Notion* as his magnum opus. At school and at college he was an excellent sportsman; a champion record-setting wrestler in Oregon. During his young years, Kesey led a bohemian way of life, was subject to drug abuse, and even imprisoned for five months for marijuana possession. After 1965 Kesey led a secluded, family-oriented lifestyle with his wife and four children for the rest of his life, teaching at the University of Oregon, from which he himself graduated in 1957.

Task 1. Sum up, as a group, what literary features are characteristic of postmodernism.

Task 2. Find out some titles of the books written by enumerated authors of postmodernist style.

Task 3. Make a table of John Updike's life and creative activity to tell about it in class. Find out what peculiarities of literary style he developed.

Task 4. Make a table of Ken Kesey's life and creative activity to tell about it in class. Get acquainted with the contents of his novel *One Flew Over the Cuckoo's Nest* to share in class.

(to Ray Bradbury)

Task 1. Find out what education Bradbury got and how it influenced his further life and career.

Task 2. Make a table of Bradbury's life and creative activity to tell about him in class. What are his most famous works? Which of them have you heard about before?

Task 3. In pairs, choose your favourite book by Bradbury and exchange your preferences in class. Task 4. Learn more about Bradbury's activity as a screenwriter. Have you seen any of his films?

Task 5. At home, read the full version of the story *A Sound of Thunder*. In pairs, explore its literary style. Exchange your opinions as a group as to what made it so popular and enduring. Write an essay expressing your opinion about the butterfly effect..

Task 6. Make illustrations to the story *A Sound of Thunder* for the class exhibition of the drawings devoted to Bradbury's creative work.

Task 7. Choose a work by Bradbury to retell it to your peers at a summer camp to evoke their interest.

(August 22, 1920 – June 5, 2012)

Bradbury was an American author and screenwriter, who worked in a variety of genres, including fantasy, science fiction, horror, detective, and mystery fiction.

Bradbury was born in Waukegan, Illinois, into an English-Swedish family, which settled in Los Angeles, California, in 1934. The boy was happy because he was in love with theatre and Hollywood. He attended Los Angeles High School and its Poetry and Drama Clubs, and often roller-skated through Hollywood, hoping to meet celebrities. He was a passionate reader and began writing his own stories at the age of eleven, influenced by Herbert Wells, Jules Verne and Edgar Poe. His first story was published in1938.

Bradbury did not go to university; he used to say that he got all his education from libraries. He even willed his personal library to the Public Library of his home town as he had read and studied a lot there. In 1947, Bradbury married Marguerite McClure and they had four daughters.

Because of his poor eyesight, Bradbury was rejected admission into the army during World War II. He became a full-time writer in 1944. The first collection of short stories, *Dark Carnival*, appeared in 1947. In 1950 he published *The Martian Chronicles*, which is a novel made up of a number of short stories; in 1951 – *The Illustrated Man*. The story *A Sound of Thunder* (1952) illustrates the idea that tiny alternations to the distant past may snowball into catastrophic changes in history (the butterfly effect). His landmark novel *Fahrenheit 451* appeared in 1953. It presents a future society where books are outlawed and "firemen" burn any that are found. Fahrenheit 451 is the temperature at which book paper catches fire, and burns.

Many of his stories are set in Green Town, a symbol of safety and home; actually, it is the artistic portrayal of his native town, Waukegan. The first of them was *Dandelion Wine* (1957).

In 1982 Bradbury said, "People ask me to predict the Future, when all I want to do is prevent it."

Bradbury wrote 27 novels and over 600 short stories, translated into 36 languages. He also wrote numerous screenplays and television scripts. Bradbury brought "modern science fiction into the literary mainstream," *The New York Times* noted about him.

A Cask of Amontillado
BY EDGAR ALLAN POE

The thousand injuries of Fortunato I had borne as I best could, but when he ventured upon insult I vowed revenge. You, who so well know the nature of my soul, will not suppose, however, that gave utterance to a threat. At length I would be avenged; this was a point definitely, settled --but the very definitiveness with which it was resolved precluded the idea of risk. I must not only punish but punish with impunity. A wrong is unredressed when retribution overtakes its redresser. It is equally unredressed when the avenger fails to make himself felt as such to him who has done the wrong. It must be understood that neither by word nor deed had I given Fortunato cause to doubt my good will. I continued, as was my in to smile in his face, and he did not perceive that my to smile now was atthe thought of his immolation.

He had a weak point --this Fortunato --although in other regards he was a man to be respected and even feared. He prided himself on his connoisseurship in wine. Few Italians have the true virtuoso spirit. For the most part their enthusiasm is adopted to suit the time and opportunity, to practise imposture upon the British and Austrian millionaires. In painting and gemmary, Fortunato, like his countrymen, was a quack, but in the matter of old wines he was sincere. In this respect I did not differ from him materially; --I was skilful in the Italian vintages myself, and bought largely whenever I could. It was about dusk, one evening during the supreme madness of the carnival season, that I encountered my friend. He accosted me with excessive warmth, for he had been drinking much. The man wore motley. He had on a tight-fitting parti-striped dress, and his head was surmounted by the conical cap and bells. I was so pleased to see him that I thought I should never have done wringing his hand. I said to him --"My dear Fortunato, you are luckily met. How remarkably well you are looking to-day. But I have received a pipeof what passes for Amontillado, and I have my doubts."

"How?" said he. "Amontillado, A pipe? Impossible! And in the middle of the carnival!""I have my doubts," I replied; "and I was silly enough to pay the full Amontillado price without consulting you in the matter. You were not to be found, and I was fearful of losing a bargain." "Amontillado!" "I have my doubts." "Amontillado!" "And I must satisfy them." "Amontillado!" "As you are engaged, I am on my way to Luchresi. If any one has a critical turn it is he. He will tell me --" "Luchresi cannot tell Amontillado from Sherry." "And yet some fools will have it that his taste is a match for your own. "Come, let us go." "Whither?" "To your vaults." "My friend, no; I will not impose upon your good nature. I perceive you have an engagement. Luchresi--" "I have no engagement; --come." "My friend, no. It is not the engagement, but the severe cold with which I perceive you are afflicted. The vaults are insufferably damp. They are encrusted with nitre." "Let us go, nevertheless. The cold is merely nothing. Amontillado! You have been imposed upon. And as for Luchresi, he cannot distinguish Sherry from Amontillado." Thus speaking, Fortunato possessed himself of my arm; and putting on a mask of black silk and drawing a roquelaire closely about my person, I suffered him to hurry me to my palazzo

There were no attendants at home; they had absconded to make merry in honour of the time. I had told them that I should not return until the morning, and had given them explicit orders not to stir from the house. These orders were sufficient, I well knew, to insure their immediate disappearance, one and all, as soon as my back was turned. I took from their sconces two flambeaux, and giving one to Fortunato, bowed him through several suites of rooms to the archway that led into the vaults. I passed down a long and winding staircase, requesting him to be cautious as he followed. We came at length to the foot of the descent, and stood together upon the damp ground of the catacombs of the Montresors. The gait of my friend was unsteady, and the bells upon his cap jingled as he strode. "The pipe," he said. "It is farther on," said I; "but observe the white web-work which gleams from these cavern walls." He turned towards me, and looked into my eves with two filmy orbs that distilled the rheum of intoxication.

"Nitre?" he asked, at length. "Nitre," I replied. "How long have you had that cough?" "Ugh! ugh! ugh! --ugh! ugh! ugh! --ugh! ugh! ugh! --ugh! ugh! ugh! --ugh! ugh! ugh!" My poor friend found it impossible to reply for many minutes. "It is nothing," he said, at last. "Come," I said, with decision, "we will go back; your health is precious. You are rich, respected, admired, beloved; you are happy, as once I was. You are a man to be missed. For me it is no matter. We will go back; you will be ill, and I cannot be responsible. Besides, there is Luchresi --" "Enough," he said; "the cough's a mere nothing; it will not kill me. I shall not die of a cough." "True --true," I replied; "and, indeed, I had no intention of alarming you unnecessarily --but you should use all proper caution. A draught of this Medoc will defend us from the damps." Here I knocked off the neck of a bottle which I drew from a long row of its fellows that lay upon the mould.

"Drink," I said, presenting him the wine. He raised it to his lips with a leer. He paused and nodded to me familiarly, while his bells jingled. "I drink," he said, "to the buried that repose around us." "And I to your long life." He again took my arm, and we proceeded. "These vaults," he said, "are extensive." "The Montresors," I replied, "were a great and numerous family." "I forget your arms." "A huge human foot d'or, in a field azure; the foot crushes a serpent rampant whose fangs are imbedded in the heel." "And the motto?" "Nemo me impune lacessit." "Good!" he said. The wine sparkled in his eyes and the bells jingled. My own fancy grew warm with the Medoc. We had passed through long walls of piled skeletons, with casks and puncheons intermingling, into the inmost recesses of the catacombs. I paused again, and this time I made bold to seize Fortunato by an arm above the elbow.

"The nitre!" I said; "see, it increases. It hangs like moss upon the vaults. We are below the river's bed. The drops of moisture trickle among the bones. Come, we will go back ere it is too late. Your cough --" "It is nothing," he said; "let us go on. But first, another draught of the Medoc." I broke and reached him a flagon of De Grave. He emptied it at a breath. His eyes flashed with a fierce light. He laughed and threw the bottle upwards with a gesticulation I did not understand. I looked at him in surprise. He repeated the movement --a grotesque one. "You do not comprehend?" he said. "Not I," I replied. "Then you are not of the brotherhood." "How?" "You are not of the masons." "Yes, yes," I said; "yes, yes." "You? Impossible! A mason?" "A mason," I replied. "A sign," he said, "a sign." "It is this," I answered, producing from beneath the folds of my roquelaire a trowel. "You jest," he exclaimed, recoiling a few paces. "But let us proceed to the Amontillado.""Be it so," I said, replacing the tool beneath the cloak and again offering him my arm. He leaned upon it heavily. We continued our route in search of the Amontillado. We passed through a range of low arches, descended, passed on, and descending again, arrived at a deep crypt, in which the foulness of the air caused our flambeaux rather to glow than flame.

At the most remote end of the crypt there appeared another less spacious. Its walls had been lined with human remains, piled to the vault overhead, in the fashion of the great catacombs of Paris. Three sides of this interior crypt were still ornamented in this manner. From the fourth side the bones had been thrown down, and lay promiscuously upon the earth, forming at one point a mound of some size. Within the wall thus exposed by the displacing of the bones, we perceived a still interior crypt or recess, in depth about four feet, in width three, in height six or seven. It seemed to have been constructed for no especial use within itself, but formed merely the interval between two of the colossal supports of the roof of the catacombs, and was backed by one of their circumscribing walls of solid granite.

It was in vain that Fortunato, uplifting his dull torch, endeavoured to pry into the depth of the recess. Its termination the feeble light did not enable us to see. "Proceed," I said; "herein is the Amontillado. As for Luchresi --" "He is an ignoramus," interrupted my friend, as he stepped unsteadily forward, while I followed immediately at his heels. In niche, and finding an instant he had reached the extremity of the niche, and finding his progress arrested by the rock, stood stupidly bewildered. A moment more and I had fettered him to the granite. In its surface were two iron staples, distant from each other about two feet, horizontally. From one of these depended a short chain, from the other a padlock. Throwing the links about his waist, it was but the work of a few seconds to secure it. He was too much astounded to resist. Withdrawing the key I stepped back from the recess. "Pass your hand," I said, "over the wall; you cannot help feeling the nitre.

Indeed, it is very damp. Once more let me implore you to return. No? Then I must positively leave you. But I must first render you all the little attentions in my power." "The Amontillado!" ejaculated my friend, not yet recovered from his astonishment. "True," I replied; "the Amontillado."

As I said these words I busied myself among the pile of bones of which I have before spoken. Throwing them aside, I soon uncovered a quantity of building stone and mortar. With these materials and with the aid of my trowel, I began vigorously to wall up the entrance of the niche. I had scarcely laid the first tier of the masonry when I discovered that the intoxication of Fortunato had in a great measure worn off. The earliest indication I had of this was a low moaning cry from the depth of the recess. It was not the cry of a drunken man. There was then a long and obstinate silence. I laid the second tier, and the third, and the fourth; and then I heard the furious vibrations of the chain. The noise lasted for several minutes, during which, that I might hearken to it with the more satisfaction, I ceased my labours and sat down upon the bones. When at last the clanking subsided, I resumed the trowel, and finished without interruption the fifth, the sixth, and the seventh tier. The wall was now nearly upon a level with my breast. I again paused, and holding the flambeaux over the mason-work, threw a few feeble rays upon the figure within. A succession of loud and shrill screams, bursting suddenly from the throat of the chained form, seemed to thrust me violently back. For a brief moment I hesitated, I trembled. Unsheathing my rapier, I began to grope with it about the recess; but the thought of an instant reassured me. I placed my hand upon the solid fabric of the catacombs, and felt satisfied. I reapproached the wall; I replied to the yells of him who clamoured. I re-echoed, I aided, I surpassed them in volume and in strength. I did this, and the clamourer grew still.

It was now midnight, and my task was drawing to a close. I had completed the eighth, the ninth and the tenth tier. I had finished a portion of the last and the eleventh; there remained but a single stone to be fitted and plastered in. I struggled with its weight; I placed it partially in its destined position. But now there came from out the niche a low laugh that erected the hairs upon my head. It was succeeded by a sad voice, which I had difficulty in recognizing as that of the noble Fortunato.

The voice said-- "Ha! ha! ha! --he! he! he! --a very good joke, indeed --an excellent jest. We will have many a rich laugh about it at the palazzo --he! he! he! --over our wine --he! he! he!" "The Amontillado!" I said. "He! he! he! --he! he! he! --yes, the Amontillado. But is it not getting late? Will not they be awaiting us at the palazzo, the Lady Fortunato and the rest? Let us be gone." "Yes," I said, "let us be gone." "For the love of God, Montresor!" "Yes," I said, "for the love of God!" But to these words I hearkened in vain for a reply. I grew impatient. I called aloud -- "Fortunato!" No answer. I called again -- "Fortunato!" No answer still. I thrust a torch through the remaining aperture and let it fall within. There came forth in return only a jingling of the bells. My heart grew sick; it was the dampness of the catacombs that made it so. I hastened to make an end of my labour. I forced the last stone into its position; I plastered it up. Against the new masonry I re-erected the old rampart of bones. For the half of a century no mortal has disturbed them. In pace requiescat!

The Salinas Valley is in Northern California. It is a long narrow swale between two ranges of mountains, and the Salinas River winds and twists up the center until it falls at last into Monterey Bay.

I remember my childhood names for grasses and secret flowers. I remember where a toad may live and what time the birds awaken in the summer—and what trees and seasons smelled like—how people looked and walked and smelled even. The memory of odors is very rich.

I remember that the Gabilan Mountains to the east of the valley were light gay mountains full of sun and loveliness and a kind of invitation, so that you wanted to climb into their warm foothills almost as you want to climb into the lap of a beloved mother. They were beckoning mountains with a brown grass love. The Santa Lucias stood up against the sky to the west and kept the valley from the open sea, and they were dark and brooding—unfriendly and dangerous. I always found in myself a dread of west and a love of east. Where I ever got such an idea I cannot say, unless it could be that the morning came over the peaks of the Gabilans and the night drifted back from the ridges of the Santa Lucias. It may be that the birth and death of the day had some part in my feeling about the two ranges of mountains.

From both sides of the valley little streams slipped out of the hill canyons and fell into the bed of the Salinas River. In the winter of wet years the streams ran full-freshet, and they swelled the river until sometimes it raged and boiled, bank full, and then it was a destroyer. The river tore the edges of the farm lands and washed whole acres down; it toppled barns and houses into itself, to go floating and bobbing away. It trapped cows and pigs and sheep and drowned them in its muddy brown water and carried them to the sea. Then when the late spring came, the river drew in from its edges and the sand banks appeared. And in the summer the river didn't run at all above ground. Some pools would be left in the deep swirl places under a high bank. The tules and grasses grew back, and willows straightened up with the flood debris in their upper branches. The Salinas was only a part-time river. The summer sun drove it underground. It was not a fine river at all, but it was the only one we had and so we boasted about it—how dangerous it was in a wet winter and how dry it was in a dry summer. You can boast about anything if it's all you have. Maybe the less you have, the more you are required to boast.

The floor of the Salinas Valley, between the ranges and below the foothills, is level because this valley used to be the bottom of a hundred-mile inlet from the sea. The river mouth at Moss Landing was centuries ago the entrance to this long inland water. Once, fifty miles down the valley, my father bored a well. The drill came up first with topsoil and then with gravel and then with white sea sand full of shells and even pieces of whalebone. There were twenty feet of sand and then black earth again, and even a piece of redwood, that imperishable wood that does not rot. Before the inland sea the valley must have been a forest. And those things had happened right under our feet. And it seemed to me sometimes at night that I could feel both the sea and the redwood forest before it.

On the wide level acres of the valley the topsoil lay deep and fertile. It required only a rich winter of rain to make it break forth in grass and flowers. The spring flowers in a wet year were unbelievable. The whole valley floor, and the foothills too, would be carpeted with lupins and poppies. Once a woman told me that colored flowers would seem more bright if you added a few white flowers to give the colors definition. Every petal of blue lupin is edged with white, so that a field of lurins is more blue than you can imagine. And mixed with these were splashes of California poppies. These too are of a burning color—not orange, not gold, but if pure gold were liquid and could raise a cream, that golden cream might be like the color of the poppies. When their season was over the yellow mustard came up and grew to a great height. When my grandfather came into the valley the mustard was so tall that a man on horseback showed only his head above the yellow flowers. On the uplands the grass would be strewn with buttercups, with hen-and-chickens, with black-centered yellow violets. And a little later in the season there would be red and yellow stands of Indian paintbrush. These were the flowers of the open places exposed to the sun.

Under the live oaks, shaded and dusky, the maidenhair flourished and gave a good smell, and under the mossy banks of the water courses whole clumps of five-fingered ferns and goldy-backs hung down. Then there were harebells, tiny lanterns, cream white and almost sinful looking, and these were so rare and magical that a child, finding one, felt singled out and special all day long.

When June came the grasses headed out and turned brown, and the hills turned a brown which was not brown but a gold and saffron and red—an indescribable color. And from then on until the next rains the earth dried and the streams stopped. Cracks appeared on the level ground. The Salinas River sank under its sand. The wind blew down the valley, picking up dust and straws, and grew stronger and harsher as it went south. It stopped in the evening. It was a rasping nervous wind, and the dust particles cut into a man's skin and burned his eyes. Men working in the fields wore goggles and tied handkerchiefs around their noses to keep the dirt out.

The valley land was deep and rich, but the foothills wore only a skin of topsoil no deeper than the grass roots; and the farther up the hills you went, the thinner grew the soil, with flints sticking through, until at the brush line it was a kind of dry flinty gravel that reflected the hot sun blindingly.

I have spoken of the rich years when the rainfall was plentiful. But there were dry years too, and they put a terror on the valley. The water came in a thirty-year cycle. There would be five or six wet and wonderful years when there might be nineteen to twenty-five inches of rain, and the land would shout with grass. Then would come six or seven pretty good years of twelve to sixteen inches of rain. And then the dry years would come, and sometimes there would be only seven or eight inches of rain. The land dried up and the grasses headed out miserably a few inches high and great bare scabby places appeared in the valley. The live oaks got a crusty look and the sagebrush was gray. The land cracked and the springs dried up and the cattle listlessly nibbled dry twigs. Then the farmers and the ranchers would be filled with disgust for the Salinas Valley. The cows would grow thin and sometimes starve to death. People would have to haul water in barrels to their farms just for drinking. Some families would sell out for nearly nothing and move away. And it never failed that during the dry years the people forgot about the rich years, and during the wet years they lost all memory of the dry years. It was always that way.

From *Notes of a Native Son*
BY JAMES BALDWIN

My last night in New Jersey, a white friend from New York took me to the nearest big town, Trenton, to go to the movies and have a few drinks. As it turned out, he also saved me from, at the very least, a violent whipping. Almost every detail of that night stands out very clearly in my memory. I even remember the name of the movie we saw because its title impressed me as being so patly ironical. It was a movie about the German occupation of France, starring Maureen O'Hara and Charles Laughton and called *This Land Is Mine*. I remember the name of the diner we walked into when the movie ended: it was the "American Diner." When we walked in the counterman asked what we wanted and I remember answering with the casual sharpness which had become my habit: "We want a hamburger and a cup of coffee, what do you think we want?" I do not know why, after a year of such rebuffs, I so completely failed to anticipate his answer, which was, of course, "We don't serve Negroes here." This reply failed to discompose me, at least for the moment. I made some sardonic comment about the name of the diner and we walked out into the streets.

This was the time of what was called the "brown-out," when the lights in all American cities were very dim. When we re-entered the streets something happened to me which had the force of an optical illusion, or a nightmare. The streets were very crowded and I was facing north. People were moving in every direction but it seemed to me, in that instant, that all of the people I could see, and many more than that, were moving toward me, against me, and that everyone was white. I remember how their faces gleamed. And I felt, like a physical sensation, a click at the nape of my neck as though some interior string connecting my head to my body had been cut. I began to walk. I heard my friend call after me, but I ignored him. Heaven only knows what was going on in his mind, but he had the good sense not to touch me—I don't know what would have happened if he had—and to keep me in sight. I don't know what was going on in my mind, either; I certainly had no conscious plan. I wanted to do something to crush

87

these white faces, which were crushing me. I walked for perhaps a block or two until I came to an enormous, glittering, and fashionable restaurant in which I knew not even the intercession of the Virgin would cause me to be served. I pushed through the doors and took the first vacant seat I saw, at a table for two, and waited.

I do not know how long I waited and I rather wonder, until today, what I could possibly have looked like. Whatever I looked like, I frightened the waitress who shortly appeared, and the moment she appeared all of my fury flowed towards her. I hated her for her white face, and for her great, astounded, frightened eyes. I felt that if she found a black man so frightening I would make her fright worth-while.

She did not ask me what I wanted, but repeated, as though she had learned it somewhere, "We don't serve Negroes here." She did not say it with the blunt, derisive hostility to which I had grown so accustomed, but, rather, with a note of apology in her voice, and fear. This made me colder and more murderous than ever. I felt I had to do something with my hands. I wanted her to come close enough for me to get her neck between my hands.

So I pretended not to have understood her, hoping to draw her closer. And she did step a very short step closer, with her pencil poised incongruously over her pad, and repeated the formula: "... don't serve Negroes here."

Somehow, with the repetition of that phrase, which was already ringing in my head like a thousand bells of a nightmare, I realized that she would never come any closer and that I would have to strike from a distance. There was nothing on the table but an ordinary water-mug half full of water, and I picked this up and hurled it with all my strength at her. She ducked and it missed her and shattered against the mirror behind the bar. And, with that sound, my frozen blood abruptly thawed, I returned from wherever I had been, I saw, for the first time, the restaurant, the people with their mouths open, already, as it seemed to me, rising as one man, and I realized what I had done, and where I was, and I was frightened. I rose and began running for the door. A round, potbellied man grabbed me by the nape of the neck just as I reached the doors and began to beat me about the face. I kicked him and got loose and ran into the streets. My friend whispered, "Run!" and I ran.

My friend stayed outside the restaurant long enough to misdirect my pursuers and the police, who arrived, he told me, at once. I do not know what I said to him when he came to my room that night. I could not have said much. I felt, in the oddest, most awful way, that I had somehow betrayed him. I lived it over and over and over again, the way one relives an automobile accident after it has happened and one finds oneself alone and safe. I could not get over two facts, both equally difficult for the imagination to grasp, and one was that I could have been murdered. But the other was that I had been ready to commit murder. I saw nothing very clearly but I did see this: that my life, my real life, was in danger, and not from anything other people might do but from the hatred I carried in my own heart.

A Sound of Thunder
BY RAY DOUGLASS BRADBURY

The sign on the wall seemed to quaver under a film of sliding warm water. Eckels felt his eyelids blink over his stare, and the sign burned in this momentary darkness:

TIME SAFARI, INC.

SAFARIS TO ANY YEAR IN THE PAST.

YOU NAME THE ANIMAL.

WE TAKE YOU THERE.

YOU SHOOT IT.

Warm phlegm gathered in Eckels' throat; he swallowed and pushed it down. The muscles around his mouth formed a smile as he put his hand slowly out upon the air, and in that hand waved a check for ten thousand dollars to the man behind the desk.

"Does this safari guarantee I come back alive?"

"We guarantee nothing," said the official, "except the dinosaurs." He turned. "This is Mr. Travis, your Safari Guide in the Past. He'll tell you what and where to shoot. If he says no shooting, no shooting. If you disobey instructions, there's a stiff penalty of another ten thousand dollars, plus possible government action, on your return."

Eckels glanced across the vast office at a mass and tangle, a snaking and humming of wires and steel boxes, at an aurora that flickered now orange, now silver, now blue. There was a sound like a gigantic bonfire burning all of Time, all the years and all the parchment calendars, all the hours piled high and set aflame.

A touch of the hand and this burning would, on the instant, beautifully reverse itself. Eckels remembered the wording in the advertisements to the letter. Out of chars and ashes, out of dust and coals, like golden salamanders, the old years, the green years, might leap; roses sweeten the air, white hair turn Irish-black, wrinkles vanish; all, everything fly back to seed, flee death, rush down to their beginnings, suns rise in western skies and set in glorious easts, moons eat themselves opposite to the custom, all and everything cupping one in another like Chinese boxes, rabbits into hats, all and everything returning to the fresh death, the seed death, the green death, to the time before the beginning. A touch of a hand might do it, the merest touch of a hand.

"Unbelievable." Eckels breathed, the light of the Machine on his thin face. "A real Time Machine." He shook his head. "Makes you think, If the election had gone badly yesterday, I might be here now running away from the results. Thank God Keith won. He'll make a fine President of the United States."

"Yes," said the man behind the desk. "We're lucky. If Deutscher had gotten in, we'd have the worst kind of dictatorship. There's an anti everything man for you, a militarist, anti-Christ, anti-human, anti-intellectual. People called us up, you know, joking but not joking. Said if Deutscher became President they wanted to go live in 1492. Of course it's not our business to conduct Escapes, but to form Safaris. Anyway, Keith's President now. All you got to worry about is-"

"Shooting my dinosaur," Eckels finished it for him.

"A Tyrannosaurus Rex. The Tyrant Lizard, the most incredible monster in history. Sign this release. Anything happens to you, we're not responsible. Those dinosaurs are hungry."

Eckels flushed angrily. "Trying to scare me!"

"Frankly, yes. We don't want anyone going who'll panic at the first shot. Six Safari leaders were killed last year, and a dozen hunters. We're here to give you the severest thrill a real hunter ever asked for. Traveling you back sixty million years to bag the biggest game in all of Time. Your personal check's still there. Tear it up."Mr. Eckels looked at the check. His fingers twitched.

"Good luck," said the man behind the desk. "Mr. Travis, he's all yours."

They moved silently across the room, taking their guns with them, toward the Machine, toward the silver metal and the roaring light.

First a day and then a night and then a day and then a night, then it was day-night-day-night. A week, a month, a year, a decade! A.D. 2055. A.D. 2019. 1999! 1957! Gone! The Machine roared.

They put on their oxygen helmets and tested the intercoms.

Eckels swayed on the padded seat, his face pale, his jaw stiff. He felt the trembling in his arms and he looked down and found his hands tight on the new rifle. There were four other men in the Machine. Travis, the Safari Leader, his assistant, Lesperance, and two other hunters, Billings and Kramer. They sat looking at each other, and the years blazed around them.

"Can these guns get a dinosaur cold?" Eckels felt his mouth saying.

"If you hit them right," said Travis on the helmet radio. "Some dinosaurs have two brains, one in the head, another far down the spinal column. We stay away from those. That's stretching luck. Put your first two shots into the eyes, if you can, blind them, and go back into the brain."

The Machine howled. Time was a film run backward. Suns fled and ten million moons fled after them. "Think," said Eckels. "Every hunter that ever lived would envy us today. This makes Africa seem like Illinois."

The Machine slowed; its scream fell to a murmur. The Machine stopped.

The sun stopped in the sky.

The fog that had enveloped the Machine blew away and they were in an old time, a very old time indeed, three hunters and two Safari Heads with their blue metal guns across their knees.

"Christ isn't born yet," said Travis, "Moses has not gone to the mountains to talk with God. The Pyramids are still in the earth, waiting to be cut out and put up. Remember that.

Alexander, Caesar, Napoleon, Hitler-none of them exists." The man nodded.

"That" - Mr. Travis pointed - "is the jungle of sixty million two thousand and fifty-five years before President Keith."

He indicated a metal path that struck off into green wilderness, over streaming swamp, among giant ferns and palms.

"And that," he said, "is the Path, laid by Time Safari for your use,

It floats six inches above the earth. Doesn't touch so much as one grass blade, flower, or tree. It's an anti-gravity metal. Its purpose is to keep you from touching this world of the past in any way. Stay on the Path. Don't go off it. I repeat. Don't go off. For any reason! If you fall off, there's a penalty. And don't shoot any animal we don't okay."

"Why?" asked Eckels.

They sat in the ancient wilderness. Far birds' cries blew on a wind, and the smell of tar and an old salt sea, moist grasses, and flowers the color of blood.

"We don't want to change the Future. We don't belong here in the Past. The government doesn't like us here. We have to pay big graft to keep our franchise. A Time Machine is finicky business. Not knowing it, we might kill an important animal, a small bird, a roach, a flower even, thus destroying an important link in a growing species."

"That's not clear," said Eckels.

"All right," Travis continued, "say we accidentally kill one mouse here. That means all the future families of this one particular mouse are destroyed, right?"

"Right"

"And all the families of the families of the families of that one mouse! With a stamp of your foot, you annihilate first one, then a dozen, then a thousand, a million, a billion possible mice!"

"So they're dead," said Eckels. "So what?"

"So what?" Travis snorted quietly. "Well, what about the foxes that'll need those mice to survive? For want of ten mice, a fox dies. For want of ten foxes a lion starves. For want of a lion, all manner of insects, vultures, infinite billions of life forms are thrown into chaos and destruction. Eventually it all boils down to this: fifty-nine million years later, a caveman, one of a dozen on the entire world, goes hunting wild boar or saber-toothed tiger for food. But you, friend, have stepped on all the tigers in that region. By stepping on one single mouse. So the caveman starves. And the caveman, please note, is not just any expendable man, no! He is an entire future nation. From his loins would have sprung ten sons. From their loins one hundred sons, and thus onward to a civilization. Destroy this one man, and you destroy a race, a people, an entire history of life. It is comparable to slaying some of Adam's grandchildren. The stomp of your foot, on one mouse, could start an earthquake, the effects of which could shake our earth and destinies down through Time, to their very foundations. With the death of that one caveman, a billion others yet unborn are throttled in the womb. Perhaps Rome never rises on its seven hills. Perhaps Europe is forever a dark forest, and only Asia waxes healthy and teeming. Step on a mouse and you crush the Pyramids. Step on a mouse and you leave your print, like a Grand Canyon, across Eternity. Queen Elizabeth might never be born, Washington might not cross the Delaware, there might never be a United States at all. So be careful. Stay on the Path. Never step off!"

"I see," said Eckels. "Then it wouldn't pay for us even to touch the grass?"

"Correct. Crushing certain plants could add up infinitesimally. A little error here would multiply in sixty million years, all out of proportion. Of course maybe our theory is wrong. Maybe Time can't be changed by us. Or maybe it can be changed only in little subtle ways. A dead mouse here makes an insect imbalance there, a population disproportion later, a bad harvest further on, a depression, mass starvation, and finally, a change in social temperament in far-flung countries. Something much more subtle, like that. Perhaps only a soft breath, a whisper, a hair, pollen on the air, such a slight, slight change that unless you looked close you wouldn't see it. Who knows? Who really can say he knows? We don't know. We're guessing. But until we do know for certain whether our messing around in Time can make a big roar or a little rustle in history, we're being careful. This Machine, this Path, your clothing and bodies, were sterilized, as you know, before the journey. We wear these oxygen helmets so we can't introduce our bacteria into an ancient atmosphere."

"How do we know which animals to shoot?"

"They're marked with red paint," said Travis. "Today, before our journey, we sent Lesperance here back with the Machine. He came to this particular era and followed certain animals."

"Studying them?"

"Right," said Lesperance. "I track them through their entire existence, noting which of them lives longest. Very few. How many times they mate. Not often. Life's short, When I find one that's going to die when a tree falls on him, or one that drowns in a tar pit, I note the exact hour, minute, and second. I shoot a paint bomb. It leaves a red patch on his side. We can't miss it. Then I correlate our arrival in the Past so that we meet the Monster not more than two minutes before he would have died anyway. This way, we kill only animals with no future, that are never going to mate again. You see how careful we are?"

"But if you come back this morning in Time," said Eckels eagerly, "you must've bumped into us, our Safari! How did it turn out? Was it successful? Did all of us get through-alive?"

Travis and Lesperance gave each other a look.

"That'd be a paradox," said the latter. "Time doesn't permit that sort of mess-a man meeting himself. When such occasions threaten, Time steps aside. Like an airplane hitting an air pocket. You felt the Machine jump just before we stopped? That was us passing ourselves on the way back to the Future. We saw nothing. There's no way of telling if this expedition was a success, if we got our monster, or whether all of us - meaning you, Mr. Eckels - got out alive."

Eckels smiled palely.

"Cut that," said Travis sharply. "Everyone on his feet!"

They were ready to leave the Machine.

The jungle was high and the jungle was broad and the jungle was the entire world forever and forever. Sounds like music and sounds like flying tents filled the sky, and those were pterodactyls soaring with cavernous gray wings, gigantic bats of delirium and night fever.

Eckels, balanced on the narrow Path, aimed his rifle playfully.

"Stop that!" said Travis. "Don't even aim for fun, blast you! If your guns should go off - - "

Eckels flushed. "Where's our Tyrannosaurus?"

Lesperance checked his wristwatch. "Up ahead, We'll bisect his trail in sixty seconds. Look for the red paint! Don't shoot till we give the word. Stay on the Path. Stay on the Path!"

They moved forward in the wind of morning.

"Strange," murmured Eckels. "Up ahead, sixty million years, Election Day over. Keith made President. Everyone celebrating. And here we are, a million years lost, and they don't exist. The things we worried about for months, a lifetime, not even born or thought of yet."

"Safety catches off, everyone!" ordered Travis. "You, first shot, Eckels. Second, Billings, Third, Kramer."

"I've hunted tiger, wild boar, buffalo, elephant, but now, this is it," said Eckels. "I'm shaking like a kid."

"Ah," said Travis.

Everyone stopped.

Travis raised his hand. "Ahead," he whispered. "In the mist. There he is. There's His Royal Majesty now."

The jungle was wide and full of twitterings, rustlings, murmurs, and sighs.

Suddenly it all ceased, as if someone had shut a door.

Silence.

A sound of thunder.

Out of the mist, one hundred yards away, came Tyrannosaurus Rex.

"It," whispered Eckels. "It......

"Sh!"

It came on great oiled, resilient, striding legs. It towered thirty feet above half of the trees, a great evil god, folding its delicate watchmaker's claws close to its oily reptilian chest. Each lower leg was a piston, a thousand pounds of white bone, sunk in thick ropes of muscle, sheathed over in a gleam of pebbled skin like the mail of a terrible warrior. Each thigh was a ton of meat, ivory, and steel mesh. And from the great breathing cage of the upper body those two delicate arms dangled out front, arms with hands which might pick up and examine men like toys, while the snake neck coiled. And the head itself, a ton of sculptured stone, lifted easily upon the sky. Its mouth gaped, exposing a fence of teeth like daggers. Its eyes rolled, ostrich eggs, empty of all expression save hunger. It closed its mouth in a death grin. It ran, its pelvic bones crushing aside trees and bushes, its taloned feet clawing damp earth, leaving prints six inches deep wherever it settled its weight.

It ran with a gliding ballet step, far too poised and balanced for its ten tons. It moved into a sunlit area warily, its beautifully reptilian hands feeling the air.

"Why, why," Eckels twitched his mouth. "It could reach up and grab the moon."

"Sh!" Travis jerked angrily. "He hasn't seen us yet."

"It can't be killed," Eckels pronounced this verdict quietly, as if there could be no argument. He had weighed the evidence and this was his considered opinion. The rifle in his hands seemed a cap gun. "We were fools to come. This is impossible."

"Shut up!" hissed Travis.

"Nightmare."

"Turn around," commanded Travis. "Walk quietly to the Machine. We'll remit half your fee."

"I didn't realize it would be this big," said Eckels. "I miscalculated, that's all. And now I want out."

"It sees us!"

"There's the red paint on its chest!"

The Tyrant Lizard raised itself. Its armored flesh glittered like a thousand green coins. The coins, crusted with slime, steamed. In the slime, tiny insects wriggled, so that the entire body seemed to twitch and undulate, even while the monster itself did not move. It exhaled. The stink of raw flesh blew down the wilderness.

"Get me out of here," said Eckels. "It was never like this before. I was always sure I'd come through alive. I had good guides, good safaris, and safety. This time, I figured wrong. I've met my match and admit it. This is too much for me to get hold of."

"Don't run," said Lesperance. "Turn around. Hide in the Machine."

"Yes." Eckels seemed to be numb. He looked at his feet as if trying to make them move. He gave a grunt of helplessness.

"Eckels!"

He took a few steps, blinking, shuffling.

"Not that way!"

The Monster, at the first motion, lunged forward with a terrible scream. It covered one hundred yards in six seconds. The rifles jerked up and blazed fire. A windstorm from the beast's mouth engulfed them in the stench of slime and old blood. The Monster roared, teeth glittering with sun.

The rifles cracked again, Their sound was lost in shriek and lizard thunder. The great level of the reptile's tail swung up, lashed sideways. Trees exploded in clouds of leaf and branch. The Monster twitched its jeweler's hands down to fondle at the men, to twist them in half, to crush them like berries, to cram them into its teeth and its screaming throat. Its boulderstone eyes leveled with the men. They saw themselves mirrored. They fired at the metallic eyelids and the blazing black iris,

Like a stone idol, like a mountain avalanche, Tyrannosaurus fell.

Thundering, it clutched trees, pulled them with it. It wrenched and tore the metal Path. The men flung themselves back and away. The body hit, ten tons of cold flesh and stone. The guns fired. The Monster lashed its armored tail, twitched its snake jaws, and lay still. A fount of blood spurted from its throat. Somewhere inside, a sac of fluids burst. Sickening gushes drenched the hunters. They stood, red and glistening.

The thunder faded.

The jungle was silent. After the avalanche, a green peace. After the nightmare, morning.

Billings and Kramer sat on the pathway and threw up. Travis and Lesperance stood with smoking rifles, cursing steadily. In the Time Machine, on his face, Eckels lay shivering. He had found his way back to the Path, climbed into the Machine.

Travis came walking, glanced at Eckels, took cotton gauze from a metal box, and returned to the others, who were sitting on the Path.

"Clean up."

They wiped the blood from their helmets. They began to curse too. The Monster lay, a hill of solid flesh. Within, you could hear the sighs and murmurs as the furthest chambers of it died, the organs malfunctioning, liquids running a final instant from pocket to sac to spleen, everything shutting off, closing up forever. It was like standing by a wrecked locomotive or a steam shovel at quitting time, all valves being released or levered tight. Bones cracked; the tonnage of its own flesh, off balance, dead weight, snapped the delicate forearms, caught underneath. The meat settled, quivering.

Another cracking sound. Overhead, a gigantic tree branch broke from its heavy mooring, fell. It crashed upon the dead beast with finality.

"There." Lesperance checked his watch. "Right on time. That's the giant tree that was scheduled to fall and kill this animal originally." He glanced at the two hunters. "You want the trophy picture?"

"What?"

"We can't take a trophy back to the Future. The body has to stay right here where it would have died originally, so the insects, birds, and bacteria can get at it, as they were intended to. Everything in balance. The body stays. But we can take a picture of you standing near it."

The two men tried to think, but gave up, shaking their heads.

They let themselves be led along the metal Path. They sank wearily into the Machine cushions. They gazed back at the ruined Monster, the stagnating mound, where already strange reptilian birds and golden insects were busy at the steaming armor. A sound on the floor of the Time Machine stiffened them. Eckels sat there, shivering.

"I'm sorry," he said at last.

"Get up!" cried Travis.

Eckels got up.

"Go out on that Path alone," said Travis. He had his rifle pointed, "You're not coming back in the Machine. We're leaving you here!"

Lesperance seized Travis's arm. "Wait-"

"Stay out of this!" Travis shook his hand away. "This fool nearly killed us. But it isn't that so much, no. It's his shoes! Look at them! He ran off the Path. That ruins us! We'll forfeit! Thousands of dollars of insurance! We guarantee no one leaves the Path. He left it. Oh, the fool! I'll have to report to the government. They might revoke our license to travel. Who knows what he's done to Time, to History!"

"Take it easy, all he did was kick up some dirt."

"How do we know?" cried Travis. "We don't know anything! It's all a mystery! Get out of here, Eckels!"

Eckels fumbled his shirt. "I'll pay anything. A hundred thousand dollars!"

Travis glared at Eckels' checkbook and spat. "Go out there. The Monster's next to the Path. Stick your arms up to your elbows in his mouth. Then you can come back with us."

"That's unreasonable!"

"The Monster's dead, you idiot. The bullets! The bullets can't be left behind. They don't belong in the Past; they might change anything. Here's my knife. Dig them out!"

The jungle was alive again, full of the old tremorings and bird cries. Eckels turned slowly to regard the primeval garbage dump, that hill of nightmares and terror. After a long time, like a sleepwalker he shuffled out along the Path.

He returned, shuddering, five minutes later, his arms soaked and red to the elbows. He held out his hands. Each held a number of steel bullets. Then he fell. He lay where he fell, not moving.

"You didn't have to make him do that," said Lesperance.

"Didn't I? It's too early to tell." Travis nudged the still body. "He'll live. Next time he won't go hunting game like this. Okay." He jerked his thumb wearily at Lesperance. "Switch on. Let's go home."

1492. 1776. 1812.

They cleaned their hands and faces. They changed their caking shirts and pants. Eckels was up and around again, not speaking. Travis glared at him for a full ten minutes.

"Don't look at me," cried Eckels. "I haven't done anything."

"Who can tell?"

"Just ran off the Path, that's all, a little mud on my shoes-what do you want me to do-get down and pray?"

"We might need it. I'm warning you, Eckels, I might kill you yet. I've got my gun ready."

"I'm innocent. I've done nothing!"

1999.2000.2055.

The Machine stopped.

"Get out," said Travis.

The room was there as they had left it. But not the same as they had left it. The same man sat behind the same desk. But the same man did not quite sit behind the same desk. Travis looked around swiftly. "Everything okay here?" he snapped.

"Fine. Welcome home!"

Travis did not relax. He seemed to be looking through the one high window.

"Okay, Eckels, get out. Don't ever come back." Eckels could not move.

"You heard me," said Travis. "What're you staring at?"

Eckels stood smelling of the air, and there was a thing to the air, a chemical taint so subtle, so slight, that only a faint cry of his subliminal senses warned him it was there. The colors, white, gray, blue, orange, in the wall, in the furniture, in the sky beyond the window, were . . . were . . . . And there was a feel. His flesh twitched. His hands twitched. He stood drinking the oddness with the pores of his body. Somewhere, someone must have been screaming one of those whistles that only a dog can hear. His body screamed silence in return. Beyond this room, beyond this wall, beyond this man who was not quite the same man seated at this desk that was not quite the same desk . . . lay an entire world of streets and people. What sort of world it was now, there was no telling. He could feel them moving there, beyond the walls, almost, like so many chess pieces blown in a dry wind ....

But the immediate thing was the sign painted on the office wall, the same sign he had read earlier today on first entering. Somehow, the sign had changed:

TYME SEFARI INC.

SEFARIS TU ANY YEER EN THE PAST.

YU NAIM THE ANIMALL.

WEE TAEK YU THAIR.

YU SHOOT ITT.

Eckels felt himself fall into a chair. He fumbled crazily at the thick slime on his boots. He held up a clod of dirt, trembling, "No, it can't be. Not a little thing like that. No!"

Embedded in the mud, glistening green and gold and black, was a butterfly, very beautiful and very dead.

"Not a little thing like that! Not a butterfly!" cried Eckels.

It fell to the floor, an exquisite thing, a small thing that could upset balances and knock down a line of small dominoes and then big dominoes and then gigantic dominoes, all down the years across Time. Eckels' mind whirled. It couldn't change things. Killing one butterfly couldn't be that important! Could it?

His face was cold. His mouth trembled, asking: "Who - who won the presidential election yesterday?"

The man behind the desk laughed. "You joking? You know very well. Deutscher, of course! Who else? Not that fool weakling Keith. We got an iron man now, a man with guts!" The official stopped. "What's wrong?"

Eckels moaned. He dropped to his knees. He scrabbled at the golden butterfly with shaking fingers. "Can't we," he pleaded to the world, to himself, to the officials, to the Machine, "can't we take it back, can't we make it alive again? Can't we start over? Can't we-"

He did not move. Eyes shut, he waited, shivering. He heard Travis breathe loud in the room; he heard Travis shift his rifle, click the safety catch, and raise the weapon.

There was a sound of thunder.

Ray Bradbury, "A Sound of Thunder," in R is for Rocket, (New York: Doubleday, 1952)

Hills Like White Elephants
BY ERNEST HEMINGWAY

The hills across the valley of the Ebro were long and white. On this side there was no shade and no trees and the station was between two lines of rails in the sun. Close against the side of the station there was the warm shadow of the building and a curtain, made of strings of bamboo beads, hung across the open door into the bar, to keep out flies. The American and the girl with him sat at a table in the shade, outside the building. It was very hot and the express from Barcelona would come in forty minutes. It stopped at this junction for two minutes and went to Madrid.

'What should we drink?' the girl asked. She had taken off her hat and put it on the table.

'It's pretty hot,' the man said.

'Let's drink beer.'

'Dos cervezas,' the man said into the curtain.

'Big ones?' a woman asked from the doorway.

'Yes. Two big ones.'

The woman brought two glasses of beer and two felt pads. She put the felt pads and the beer glass on the table and looked at the man and the girl. The girl was looking off at the line of hills. They were white in the sun and the country was brown and dry.

'They look like white elephants,' she said.

'I've never seen one,' the man drank his beer.

'No, you wouldn't have.'

'I might have,' the man said. 'Just because you say I wouldn't have doesn't prove anything.'

The girl looked at the bead curtain. 'They've painted something on it,' she said. 'What does it say?'

'Anis del Toro. It's a drink.'

'Could we try it?'

The man called 'Listen' through the curtain. The woman came out from the bar.

'Four reales.'

'We want two Anis del Toro.'

'With water?'

'Do you want it with water?'

'I don't know,' the girl said. 'Is it good with water?'

'It's all right.'

'You want them with water?' asked the woman.

'Yes, with water.'

'It tastes like liquorice,' the girl said and put the glass down.

'That's the way with everything.'

'Yes,' said the girl. 'Everything tastes of liquorice. Especially all the things you've waited so long for, like absinthe.'

'Oh, cut it out.'

'You started it,' the girl said. 'I was being amused. I was having a fine time.'

'Well, let's try and have a fine time.'

'All right. I was trying. I said the mountains looked like white elephants. Wasn't that bright?'

'That was bright.'

'I wanted to try this new drink. That's all we do, isn't it - look at things and try new drinks?'

'I guess so.'

The girl looked across at the hills.

'They're lovely hills,' she said. 'They don't really look like white elephants. I just meant the colouring of their skin through the trees.'

'Should we have another drink?'

'All right.'

The warm wind blew the bead curtain against the table.

'The beer's nice and cool,' the man said.

'It's lovely,' the girl said.

'It's really an awfully simple operation, Jig,' the man said. 'It's not really an operation at all.'

The girl looked at the ground the table legs rested on.

'I know you wouldn't mind it, Jig. It's really not anything. It's just to let the air in.'

The girl did not say anything.

'I'll go with you and I'll stay with you all the time. They just let the air in and then it's all perfectly natural.'

'Then what will we do afterwards?'

'We'll be fine afterwards. Just like we were before.'

'What makes you think so?'

'That's the only thing that bothers us. It's the only thing that's made us unhappy.'

The girl looked at the bead curtain, put her hand out and took hold of two of the strings of beads.

'And you think then we'll be all right and be happy.'

'I know we will. You don't have to be afraid. I've known lots of people that have done it.'

'So have I,' said the girl. 'And afterwards they were all so happy.'

'Well,' the man said, 'if you don't want to you don't have to. I wouldn't have you do it if you didn't want to. But I know it's perfectly simple.'

'And you really want to?'

'I think it's the best thing to do. But I don't want you to do it if you don't really want to.'

'And if I do it you'll be happy and things will be like they were and you'll love me?'

'I love you now. You know I love you.'

'I know. But if I do it, then it will be nice again if I say things are like white elephants, and you'll like it?'

'I'll love it. I love it now but I just can't think about it. You know how I get when I worry.'

'If I do it you won't ever worry?'

'I won't worry about that because it's perfectly simple.'

'Then I'll do it. Because I don't care about me.'

'What do you mean?'

'I don't care about me.'

'Well, I care about you.'

'Oh, yes. But I don't care about me. And I'll do it and then everything will be fine.'

'I don't want you to do it if you feel that way.'

The girl stood up and walked to the end of the station. Across, on the other side, were fields of grain and trees along the banks of the Ebro. Far away, beyond the river, were mountains. The shadow of a cloud moved across the field of grain and she saw the river through the trees.

'And we could have all this,' she said. 'And we could have everything and every day we make it more impossible.'

'What did you say?'

'I said we could have everything.'

'We can have everything.'

'No, we can't.'

'We can have the whole world.'

'No, we can't.'

'We can go everywhere.'

'No, we can't. It isn't ours any more.'

'It's ours.'

'No, it isn't. And once they take it away, you never get it back.'

'But they haven't taken it away.'

'We'll wait and see.'

'Come on back in the shade,' he said. 'You mustn't feel that way.'

'I don't feel any way,' the girl said. 'I just know things.'

'I don't want you to do anything that you don't want to do -'

'Nor that isn't good for me,' she said. 'I know. Could we have another beer?'

'All right. But you've got to realize - '

'I realize,' the girl said. 'Can't we maybe stop talking?'

They sat down at the table and the girl looked across at the hills on the dry side of the valley and the man looked at her and at the table.

'You've got to realize,' he said, ' that I don't want you to do it if you don't want to. I'm perfectly willing to go through with it if it means anything to you.'

'Doesn't it mean anything to you? We could get along.'

'Of course it does. But I don't want anybody but you. I don't want anyone else. And I know it's perfectly simple.'

'Yes, you know it's perfectly simple.'

'It's all right for you to say that, but I do know it.'

'Would you do something for me now?'

'I'd do anything for you.'

'Would you please please please please please please please stop talking?'

He did not say anything but looked at the bags against the wall of the station. There were labels on them from all the hotels where they had spent nights.

'But I don't want you to,' he said, 'I don't care anything about it.'

'I'll scream,' the girl said.

The woman came out through the curtains with two glasses of beer and put them down on the damp felt pads. 'The train comes in five minutes,' she said.

'What did she say?' asked the girl.

'That the train is coming in five minutes.'

The girl smiled brightly at the woman, to thank her.

'I'd better take the bags over to the other side of the station,' the man said. She smiled at him.

'All right. Then come back and we'll finish the beer.'

He picked up the two heavy bags and carried them around the station to the other tracks. He looked up the tracks but could not see the train. Coming back, he walked through the bar-room, where people waiting for the train were drinking. He drank an

Anis at the bar and looked at the people. They were all waiting reasonably for the train. He went out through the bead curtain. She was sitting at the table and smiled at him.

'Do you feel better?' he asked.

'I feel fine,' she said. 'There's nothing wrong with me. I feel fine.'

Every Little Hurricane
BY SHERMAN ALEXIE

Although it was winter, the nearest ocean four hundred miles away, and the Tribal Weatherman asleep because of boredom, a hurricane dropped from the sky in 1976 and fell so hard on the Spokane Indian Reservation that it knocked Victor from bed and his latest nightmare. It was January and Victor was nine years old. He was sleeping in his bedroom in the basement of the HUD house when it happened. His mother and father were upstairs, hosting the largest New Year's Eve party in tribal history, when the winds increased and the first tree fell. "Damn it," one Indian yelled at another as the argument began. "You ain't nothin', you damn apple!"

The two Indians raged across the room at each other. One was tall and heavy, the other was short, muscular. High-pressure and low-pressure fronts.

The music was so loud that Victor could barely hear the voices as the two Indians escalated the argument into a fistfight. Soon there were no voices to be heard, only guttural noises that could have been curses or wood breaking. Then the music stopped so suddenly that the silence frightened Victor.

"What the hell's going on?" Victor's father yelled, his voice coming quickly and with force. It shook the walls of the house.

"Adolph and Arnold are fighting again," Victor's mother said. Adolph and Arnold were her brothers, Victor's uncles. They always fought. Had been fighting since the very beginning.

"Well, tell them to get their damn asses out of my house," Victor's father yelled again, his decibel level rising to meet the tension in the house.

"They already left," Victor's mother said. "They're fighting out in the yard."

Victor heard this and ran to his window. He could see his uncles slugging each other with such force that they had to be in love. Strangers would never want to hurt each other that badly. But it was strangely quiet, like Victor was watching a television show with the volume turned all the way down. He could hear the party upstairs move to the windows, step onto the front porch to watch the battle.

During other hurricanes broadcast on the news, Victor had seen crazy people tie themselves to trees on the beach. Those people wanted to feel the force of the hurricane firsthand, wanted it to be like an amusement ride, but the thin ropes were broken and the people were broken. Sometimes the trees themselves were pulled from the ground and both the trees and the people tied to the trees were carried away.

Standing at his window, watching his uncles grow bloody and tired, Victor pulled the strings of his pajama bottoms tighter. He squeezed his hands into fists and pressed his face tightly against the glass.

"They're going to kill each other," somebody yelled from an upstairs window. Nobody disagreed and nobody moved to change the situation. Witnesses. They were all witnesses and nothing more. For hundreds of years, Indians were witnesses to crimes of an epic scale. Victor's uncles were in the midst of a misdemeanor that would remain one even if somebody was to die. One Indian killing another did not create a special kind of storm. This little kind of hurricane was generic. It didn't even deserve a name.

Adolph soon had the best of Arnold, though, and was trying to drown him in the snow. Victor watched as his uncle held his other uncle down, saw the look of hate and love on his uncle's face and the terrified arms of his other uncle flailing uselessly.

Then it was over.

Adolph let Arnold loose, even pulled him to his feet, and they both stood, facing each other. They started to yell again, unintelligible and unintelligent. The volume grew as other voices from the party upstairs were added. Victor could almost smell the sweat and whiskey and blood. Everybody was assessing the damage, considering options. Would the fight continue? Would it decrease in intensity until both uncles sat quietly in opposite corners, exhausted and ashamed? Could the Indian Health Service doctors fix the broken nose and sprained ankles?

But there was other pain. Victor knew that. He stood at his window and touched his own body. His legs and back hurt from a day of sledding, his head was a little sore from where he bumped into a door earlier in the week. One molar ached from cavity; his chest throbbed with absence.

Victor had seen the news footage of cities after hurricanes had passed by. Houses were flattened, their contents thrown in every direction. Memories not destroyed, but forever changed and damaged. Which is worse? Victor wanted to know if memories of his personal hurricanes would be better if he could change them. Or if he just forgot about all of it. Victor had once seen a photograph of a car that a hurricane had picked up and carried for five miles before it fell onto a house. Victor remembered everything exactly that way.

On Christmas Eve when he was five, Victor's father wept because he didn't have any money for gifts. Oh, there was a tree trimmed with ornaments, a few bulbs from the Trading Post, one string of lights, and photographs of the family with holes punched through the top, threaded with dental floss, and hung from tiny branches. But there were no gifts. Not one.

"But we've got each other," Victor's mother said, but she knew it was just dry recitation of the old Christmas movies they watched on television. It wasn't real. Victor watched his father cry huge, gasping tears. Indian tears.

Victor imagined that his father's tears could have frozen solid in the severe reservation winters and shattered when they hit the floor. Sent millions of icy knives through the air, each specific and beautiful. Each dangerous and random.

Victor imagined that he held an empty box beneath his father's eyes and collected the tears, held that box until it was full. Victor would wrap it in Sunday comics and give it to his mother.

Just the week before, Victor had stood in the shadows of his father's doorway and watched as the man had opened his wallet and shook his head. Empty. Victor watched his father put the empty wallet back in his pocket for a moment, then pull it out and open it again. Still empty. Victor watched his father repeat this ceremony again and again, as if the repetition itself could guarantee change. But it was always empty.

During all these kinds of tiny storms, Victor's mother would rise with her medicine and magic. She would pull air down from empty cupboards and make fry bread. She would shake thick blankets free from old bandanas. She would comb Victor's braids into dreams.

In those dreams, Victor and his parents would be sitting in Mother's Kitchen restaurant in Spokane, waiting out a storm. Rain and lightning. Unemployment and poverty. Commodity food. Flash floods.

"Soup," Victor's father would always say. "I want a bowl of soup."

Mother's Kitchen was always warm in those dreams. There was always a good song on the jukebox, a song that Victor didn't really know but he knew it was good. And he knew it was a song from his parents' youth. In those dreams, all was good.

Sometimes, though, the dream became a nightmare and Mother's Kitchen was out of soup, the jukebox only played country music, and the roof leaked. Rain fell like drums into buckets and pots and pans set out to catch whatever they could. In those nightmares, Victor sat in his chair as rain fell, drop by drop, onto his head.

In those nightmares, Victor felt his stomach ache with hunger. In fact, he felt his own interior sway, nearly buckle, then fall. Gravity. Nothing for dinner except sleep. Gale and unsteady barometer.

In other nightmares, in his everyday reality, Victor watched his father take a drink of vodka on a completely empty stomach. Victor could hear that near-poison fall, then hit, flesh and blood, nerve and vein. Maybe it was like lightning tearing an old tree into halves. Maybe it was like a wall of water, a reservation tsunami, crashing onto a small beach. Maybe it was like Hiroshima or Nagasaki. Maybe it was like all that. Maybe. But after he drank, Victor's father would breathe in deep and close his eyes, stretch, and straighten his neck and back. During those long drinks, Victor's father wasn't shaped like a question mark. He looked more like an exclamation point.

Some people liked the rain. But Victor hated it. Really hated it. The damp. Humidity. Low clouds and lies. Weathermen.

When it was raining, Victor would apologize to everyone he talked to.

"Sorry about the weather," he would say.

Once, Victor's cousins made him climb a tall tree during a rainstorm. The bark was slick, nearly impossible to hold on to, but Victor kept climbing. The branches kept most of the rain off him, but there were always sudden funnels of water that broke through, startling enough to nearly make Victor lose his grip. Sudden rain like promises, like treaties. But Victor held on.

There was so much that Victor feared, so much his intense imagination created. For years, Victor feared that he was going to drown while it was raining, so that even when he thrashed through the lake and opened his mouth to scream, he would taste even more water falling from the sky. Sometimes he was sure that he would fall from the top of the slide or from a swing and a whirlpool would suddenly appear beneath him and carry him down into the earth, drown him at the core.

And of course, Victor dreamed of whiskey, vodka, tequila, those fluids swallowing him just as easily as he swallowed them. When he was five years old, an old Indian man drowned in a mud puddle at the powwow. Just passed out and fell facedown into the water collected in a tire track. Even at five, Victor understood what that meant, how it defined nearly everything. Fronts. Highs and lows. Thermals and undercurrents. Tragedy.

When the hurricane descended on the reservation in 1976, Victor was there to record it. If the video camera had been available then, Victor might have filmed it, but his memory was much more dependable.

His uncles, Arnold and Adolph, gave up the fight and walked back into the house, into the New Year's Eve party, arms linked, forgiving each other. But the storm that had caused their momentary anger had not died. Instead, it moved from Indian to Indian at the party, giving each a specific, painful memory.

Victor's father remembered the time his own father was spit on as they waited for a bus in Spokane.

Victor's mother remembered how the Indian Health Service doctor sterilized her moments after Victor was born.

Adolph and Arnold were touched by memories of previous battles, storms that continually haunted their lives. When children grow up together in poverty, a bond is formed that is stronger than most anything. It's this same bond that causes so much pain. Adolph and Arnold reminded each other of their childhood, how they had crackers in their shared bedroom so they would have something to eat.

"Did you hide those crackers?" Adolph asked his brother so many times that he still whispered that question in his sleep.

Other Indians at the party remembered their own pain. This pain grew, expanded. One person lost her temper when she accidentally brushed the skin of another. The forecast was not good. Indians continued to drink, harder and harder, as if anticipating. There's a fifty percent chance of torrential rain, blizzard-like conditions, seismic activity. Then there's a sixty percent chance, then seventy, eighty.

Victor was back in his bed, lying flat and still, watching the ceiling lower with each step above. The ceiling lowered with the weight of each Indian's pain, until it was just inches from

Victor's nose. He wanted to scream, wanted to pretend it was just a nightmare or a game invented by his parents to help him sleep.

The voices upstairs continued to grow, take shape and fill space until Victor's room, the entire house, was consumed by the party. Until Victor crawled from his bed and went to find his parents.

"Ya-hey, little nephew," Adolph said as Victor stood alone in a corner.

"Hello, Uncle," Victor said and gave Adolph a hug, gagged at his smell. Alcohol and sweat. Cigarettes and failure.

"Where's my dad?" Victor asked.

"Over there," Adolph said and waved his arm in the general direction of the kitchen. The house was not very large, but there were so many people and so much emotion filling the spaces between people that it was like a maze for little Victor. No matter which way he turned, he could not find his father or mother.

"Where are they?" he asked his aunt Nezzy. "Who?" she asked.

"Mom and Dad," Victor said, and Nezzy pointed toward the bedroom. Victor made his way through the crowd, hated his tears. He didn't hate the fear and pain that caused them. He expected that. What he hated was the way they felt against his cheeks, his chin, his skin as they made their way down his face. Victor cried until he found his parents, alone, passed out on their bed in the back bedroom.

Victor climbed up on the bed and lay down between them. His mother and father breathed deep, nearly choking alcoholic snores. They were sweating although the room was cold, and Victor thought the alcohol seeping through their skin might get him drunk, might help him sleep. He kissed his mother's neck, tasted the salt and whiskey. He kissed his father's forearm, tasted the cheap beer and smoke.

Victor closed his eyes tightly. He said his prayers just in case his parents had been wrong about God all those years. He listened for hours to every little hurricane spun from the larger hurricane that battered the reservation.

During that night, his aunt Nezzy broke her arm when an unidentified Indian woman pushed her down the stairs. Eugene Boyd broke a door playing indoor basketball. Lester Falls Apart passed out on the stove and somebody turned the burners on high. James Many Horses sat in the corner and told so many bad jokes that three or four Indians threw him out the door into the snow.

"How do you get one hundred Indians to yell, Oh, crap?" James Many Horses asked as he sat in a drift on the front lawn. "Say Bingo," James Many Horses answered himself when nobody from the party would.

James didn't spend very much time alone in the snow. Soon Seymour and Lester were there, too. Seymour was thrown out because he kept flirting with all the women. Lester was there to cool off his burns. Soon everybody from the party was out on the lawn, dancing in the snow, rolling in the snow, fighting in the snow.

Victor lay between his parents, his alcoholic and dreamless parents, his mother and father. Victor licked his index finger and raised it into the air to test the wind. Velocity. Direction. Sleep approaching. The people outside seemed so far away, so strange and imaginary. There was a downshift of emotion, tension seemed to wane. Victor put one hand on his mother's stomach and placed the other on his father's. There was enough hunger in both, enough movement, enough geography and history, enough of everything to destroy the reservation and leave only random debris and broken furniture.

But it was over. Victor closed his eyes, fell asleep. It was over. The hurricane that fell out of the sky in 1976 left before sunrise, and all the Indians, the eternal survivors, gathered to count their losses.

The Last Leaf
BY O. HENRY

In a little district west of Washington Square the streets have run crazy and broken themselves into small strips called "places." These "places" make strange angles and curves. One Street crosses itself a time or two. An artist once discovered a valuable possibility in this street. Suppose a collector with a bill for paints, paper and canvas should, in traversing this route, suddenly meet himself coming back, without a cent having been paid on account!

So, to quaint old Greenwich Village the art people soon came prowling, hunting for north windows and eighteenth-century gables and Dutch attics and low rents. Then they imported some pewter mugs and a chafing dish or two from Sixth Avenue, and became a "colony."

At the top of a squatty, three-story brick Sue and Johnsy had their studio. "Johnsy" was familiar for Joanna. One was from Maine; the other from California. They had met at the table d'hôte of an Eighth Street "Delmonico's," and found their tastes in art, chicory salad and bishop sleeves so congenial that the joint studio resulted.

That was in May. In November a cold, unseen stranger, whom the doctors called Pneumonia, stalked about the colony, touching one here and there with his icy fingers. Over on the east side this ravager strode boldly, smiting his victims by scores, but his feet trod slowly through the maze of the narrow and moss-grown "places."

Mr. Pneumonia was not what you would call a chivalric old gentleman. A mite of a little woman with blood thinned by California zephyrs was hardly fair game for the red-fisted, short-breathed old duffer. But Johnsy he smote; and she lay, scarcely

113

moving, on her painted iron bedstead, looking through the small Dutch window-panes at the blank side of the next brick house.

One morning the busy doctor invited Sue into the hallway with a shaggy, grey eyebrow.

"She has one chance in - let us say, ten," he said, as he shook down the mercury in his clinical thermometer. " And that chance is for her to want to live. This way people have of lining-u on the side of the undertaker makes the entire pharmacopoeia look silly. Your little lady has made up her mind that she's not going to get well. Has she anything on her mind?"

"She - she wanted to paint the Bay of Naples some day." said Sue.

"Paint? - bosh! Has she anything on her mind worth thinking twice - a man for instance?"

"A man?" said Sue, with a jew's-harp twang in her voice. "Is a man worth - but, no, doctor; there is nothing of the kind."

"Well, it is the weakness, then," said the doctor. "I will do all that science, so far as it may filter through my efforts, can accomplish. But whenever my patient begins to count the carriages in her funeral procession I subtract 50 per cent from the curative power of medicines. If you will get her to ask one question about the new winter styles in cloak sleeves I will promise you a one-in-five chance for her, instead of one in ten."

After the doctor had gone Sue went into the workroom and cried a Japanese napkin to a pulp. Then she swaggered into Johnsy's room with her drawing board, whistling ragtime.

Johnsy lay, scarcely making a ripple under the bedclothes, with her face toward the window. Sue stopped whistling, thinking she was asleep.

She arranged her board and began a pen-and-ink drawing to illustrate a magazine story. Young artists must pave their way to Art by drawing pictures for magazine stories that young authors write to pave their way to Literature.

As Sue was sketching a pair of elegant horseshow riding trousers and a monocle of the figure of the hero, an Idaho cowboy, she heard a low sound, several times repeated. She went quickly to the bedside.

Johnsy's eyes were open wide. She was looking out the window and counting - counting backward.

"Twelve," she said, and little later "eleven"; and then "ten," and "nine"; and then "eight" and "seven", almost together.

Sue look solicitously out of the window. What was there to count? There was only a bare, dreary yard to be seen, and the blank side of the brick house twenty feet away. An old, old ivy vine, gnarled and decayed at the roots, climbed half way up the brick wall. The cold breath of autumn had stricken its leaves from the vine until its skeleton branches clung, almost bare, to the crumbling bricks.

"What is it, dear?" asked Sue.

"Six," said Johnsy, in almost a whisper. "They're falling faster now. Three days ago there were almost a hundred. It made my head ache to count them. But now it's easy. There goes another one. There are only five left now."

"Five what, dear? Tell your Sudie."

"Leaves. On the ivy vine. When the last one falls I must go, too. I've known that for three days. Didn't the doctor tell you?"

"Oh, I never heard of such nonsense," complained Sue, with magnificent scorn. "What have old ivy leaves to do with your getting well? And you used to love that vine so, you naughty girl. Don't be a goosey. Why, the doctor told me this morning that your chances for getting well real soon were - let's see exactly what he said - he said the chances were ten to one! Why, that's almost as good a chance as we have in New York when we ride on the street cars or walk past a new building. Try to take some broth now, and let Sudie go back to her drawing, so she can sell the editor man with it, and buy port wine for her sick child, and pork chops for her greedy self."

"You needn't get any more wine," said Johnsy, keeping her eyes fixed out the window. "There goes another. No, I don't want any broth. That leaves just four. I want to see the last one fall before it gets dark. Then I'll go, too."

"Johnsy, dear," said Sue, bending over her, "will you promise me to keep your eyes closed, and not look out the window until I am done working? I must hand those drawings in by to-morrow. I need the light, or I would draw the shade down."

"Couldn't you draw in the other room?" asked Johnsy, coldly.

"I'd rather be here by you," said Sue. "Beside, I don't want you to keep looking at those silly ivy leaves."

"Tell me as soon as you have finished," said Johnsy, closing her eyes, and lying white and still as fallen statue, "because I want to see the last one fall. I'm tired of waiting. I'm tired of thinking. I want to turn loose my hold on everything, and go sailing down, down, just like one of those poor, tired leaves."

"Try to sleep," said Sue. "I must call Behrman up to be my model for the old hermit miner. I'll not be gone a minute. Don't try to move 'til I come back."

Old Behrman was a painter who lived on the ground floor beneath them. He was past sixty and had a Michael Angelo's Moses beard curling down from the head of a satyr along with the body of an imp. Behrman was a failure in art. Forty years he had wielded the brush without getting near enough to touch the hem of his Mistress's robe. He had been always about to paint a masterpiece, but had never yet begun it. For several years he had painted nothing except now and then a daub in the line of commerce or advertising. He earned a little by serving as a model to those young artists in the colony who could not pay the price of a professional. He drank gin to excess, and still talked of his coming masterpiece. For the rest he was a fierce little old man, who scoffed terribly at softness in any one, and who regarded himself as especial mastiff-in-waiting to protect the two young artists in the studio above.

Sue found Behrman smelling strongly of juniper berries in his dimly lighted den below. In one corner was a blank canvas on an easel that had been waiting there for twenty-five years to receive the first line of the masterpiece. She told him of Johnsy's fancy, and how she feared she would, indeed, light and fragile as a leaf herself, float away, when her slight hold upon the world grew weaker.

Old Behrman, with his red eyes plainly streaming, shouted his contempt and derision for such idiotic imaginings.

"Vass!" he cried. "Is dere people in de world mit der foolishness to die because leafs dey drop off from a confounded vine? I haf not heard of such a thing. No, I will not bose as a model for your fool hermit-dunderhead. Vy do you allow dot silly pusiness to come in der brain of her? Ach, dot poor leetle Miss Yohnsy."

"She is very ill and weak," said Sue, "and the fever has left her mind morbid and full of strange fancies. Very well, Mr. Behrman, if you do not care to pose for me, you needn't. But I think you are a horrid old - old flibbertigibbet."

"You are just like a woman!" yelled Behrman. "Who said I will not bose? Go on. I come mit you. For half an hour I haf peen trying to say dot I am ready to bose. Gott! dis is not any blace in which one so goot as Miss Yohnsy shall lie sick. Some day I vill baint a masterpiece, and ve shall all go away. Gott! yes."

Johnsy was sleeping when they went upstairs. Sue pulled the shade down to the window-sill, and motioned Behrman into the other room. In there they peered out the window fearfully at the ivy vine. Then they looked at each other for a moment without speaking. A persistent, cold rain was falling, mingled with snow. Behrman, in his old blue shirt, took his seat as the hermit miner on an upturned kettle for a rock.

When Sue awoke from an hour's sleep the next morning she found Johnsy with dull, wide-open eyes staring at the drawn green shade.

"Pull it up; I want to see," she ordered, in a whisper.

Wearily Sue obeyed.

But, lo! after the beating rain and fierce gusts of wind that had endured through the livelong night, there yet stood out against the brick wall one ivy leaf. It was the last one on the vine. Still dark green near its stem, with its serrated edges tinted with the yellow of dissolution and decay, it hung bravely from the branch some twenty feet above the ground.

"It is the last one," said Johnsy. "I thought it would surely fall during the night. I heard the wind. It will fall to-day, and I shall die at the same time."

"Dear, dear!" said Sue, leaning her worn face down to the pillow, "think of me, if you won't think of yourself. What would I do?"

But Johnsy did not answer. The lonesomest thing in all the world is a soul when it is making ready to go on its mysterious, far journey. The fancy seemed to possess her more strongly as one by one the ties that bound her to friendship and to earth were loosed.

The day wore away, and even through the twilight they could see the lone ivy leaf clinging to its stem against the wall. And then, with the coming of the night the north wind was again loosed, while the rain still beat against the windows and pattered down from the low Dutch eaves.

When it was light enough Johnsy, the merciless, commanded that the shade be raised.

The ivy leaf was still there.

Johnsy lay for a long time looking at it. And then she called to Sue, who was stirring her chicken broth over the gas stove.

"I've been a bad girl, Sudie," said Johnsy. "Something has made that last leaf stay there to show me how wicked I was. It is a sin to want to die. You may bring a me a little broth now, and some milk with a little port in it, and - no; bring me a hand-mirror first, and then pack some pillows about me, and I will sit up and watch you cook."

And hour later she said:

"Sudie, some day I hope to paint the Bay of Naples."

The doctor came in the afternoon, and Sue had an excuse to go into the hallway as he left.

"Even chances," said the doctor, taking Sue's thin, shaking hand in his. "With good nursing you'll win." And now I must see another case I have downstairs. Behrman, his name is - some kind of an artist, I believe. Pneumonia, too. He is an old, weak man, and the attack is acute. There is no hope for him; but he goes to the hospital to-day to be made more comfortable."

The next day the doctor said to Sue: "She's out of danger. You won. Nutrition and care now - that's all."

And that afternoon Sue came to the bed where Johnsy lay, contentedly knitting a very blue and very useless woollen shoulder scarf, and put one arm around her, pillows and all.

"I have something to tell you, white mouse," she said. "Mr. Behrman died of pneumonia to-day in the hospital. He was ill only two days. The janitor found him the morning of the first day in his room downstairs helpless with pain. His shoes and clothing were wet through and icy cold. They couldn't imagine where he had been on such a dreadful night. And then they found a lantern, still lighted, and a ladder that had been dragged from its place, and some scattered brushes, and a palette with green and yellow colours mixed on it, and - look out the window, dear, at the last ivy leaf on the wall. Didn't you wonder why it never fluttered or moved when the wind blew? Ah, darling, it's Behrman's masterpiece - he painted it there the night that the last leaf fell."

In the greenest of our valleys
By good angels tenanted,
Once a fair and stately palace—
Radiant palace—reared its head.
In the monarch Thought's dominion,
It stood there!
Never seraph spread a pinion
Over fabric half so fair!

Banners yellow, glorious, golden,
On its roof did float and flow
(This—all this—was in the olden
Time long ago)
And every gentle air that dallied,
In that sweet day,
Along the ramparts plumed and pallid,
A wingèd odor went away.

Wanderers in that happy valley,
Through two luminous windows, saw
Spirits moving musically
To a lute's well-tunèd law,
Round about a throne where, sitting,
Porphyrogene!
In state his glory well befitting,
The ruler of the realm was seen.

And all with pearl and ruby glowing
Was the fair palace door,
Through which came flowing, flowing, flowing
And sparkling evermore,
A troop of Echoes, whose sweet duty
Was but to sing,
In voices of surpassing beauty,
The wit and wisdom of their king.

But evil things, in robes of sorrow,

Assailed the monarch's high estate;
(Ah, let us mourn!—for never morrow
Shall dawn upon him, desolate!)
And round about his home the glory
That blushed and bloomed
Is but a dim-remembered story
Of the old time entombed.

And travellers, now, within that valley,
Through the red-litten windows see
Vast forms that move fantastically
To a discordant melody;
While, like a ghastly rapid river,
Through the pale door
A hideous throng rush out forever,
And   laugh—but   smile   no   more.

Gaily bedight,
  A gallant knight,
In sunshine and in shadow,
  Had journeyed long,
  Singing a song,
In search of Eldorado.

  But he grew old—
  This knight so bold—
And o'er his heart a shadow—
  Fell as he found
  No spot of ground
That looked like Eldorado.

  And, as his strength
  Failed him at length,
He met a pilgrim shadow—
  'Shadow,' said he,
  'Where can it be—
This land of Eldorado?'

  'Over the Mountains
  Of the Moon,
Down the Valley of the Shadow,
  Ride, boldly ride,'
  The shade replied,—
'If you seek for Eldorado!

The Arrow and the Song
BY HENRY WADSWORTH LONGFELLOW

I shot an arrow into the air,
It fell to earth, I knew not where;
For, so swiftly it flew, the sight
Could not follow it in its flight.

I breathed a song into the air,
It fell to earth, I knew not where;
For who has sight so keen and strong,
That it can follow the flight of song?

Long, long afterward, in an oak
I found the arrow, still unbroke;
And the song, from beginning to end,
I found again in the heart of a friend.

BY HENRY WADSWORTH LONGFELLOW

As a fond mother, when the day is o'er,
Leads by the hand her little child to bed,
Half willing, half reluctant to be led,
And leave his broken playthings on the floor,
Still gazing at them through the open door,
Nor wholly reassured and comforted
By promises of others in their stead,
Which, though more splendid, may not please him more;
So Nature deals with us, and takes away
Our playthings one by one, and by the hand
Leads us to rest so gently, that we go
Scarce knowing if we wish to go or stay,
Being too full of sleep to understand
How far the unknown transcends the what we know.

Two roads diverged in a yellow wood,
And sorry I could not travel both
And be one traveler, long I stood
And looked down one as far as I could
To where it bent in the undergrowth;

Then took the other, as just as fair,
And having perhaps the better claim,
Because it was grassy and wanted wear;
Though as for that the passing there
Had worn them really about the same,

And both that morning equally lay
In leaves no step had trodden black.
Oh, I kept the first for another day!
Yet knowing how way leads on to way,
I doubted if I should ever come back.

I shall be telling this with a sigh
Somewhere ages and ages hence:
Two roads diverged in a wood, and I—
I took the one less traveled by,
And that has made all the difference.

Something there is that doesn't love a wall,
That sends the frozen-ground-swell under it,
And spills the upper boulders in the sun;
And makes gaps even two can pass abreast.
The work of hunters is another thing:
I have come after them and made repair
Where they have left not one stone on a stone,
But they would have the rabbit out of hiding,
To please the yelping dogs. The gaps I mean,
No one has seen them made or heard them made,
But at spring mending-time we find them there.
I let my neighbor know beyond the hill;
And on a day we meet to walk the line
And set the wall between us once again.
We keep the wall between us as we go.
To each the boulders that have fallen to each.
And some are loaves and some so nearly balls
We have to use a spell to make them balance:
'Stay where you are until our backs are turned!'
We wear our fingers rough with handling them.
Oh, just another kind of out-door game,
One on a side. It comes to little more:
There where it is we do not need the wall:
He is all pine and I am apple orchard.
My apple trees will never get across
And eat the cones under his pines, I tell him.
He only says, 'Good fences make good neighbors.'
Spring is the mischief in me, and I wonder
If I could put a notion in his head:
'Why do they make good neighbors? Isn't it
Where there are cows? But here there are no cows.
Before I built a wall I'd ask to know
What I was walling in or walling out,
And to whom I was like to give offense.
Something there is that doesn't love a wall,
That wants it down.' I could say 'Elves' to him,

But it's not elves exactly, and I'd rather
He said it for himself. I see him there
Bringing a stone grasped firmly by the top
In each hand, like an old-stone savage armed.
He moves in darkness as it seems to me,
Not of woods only and the shade of trees.
He will not go behind his father's saying,
And he likes having thought of it so well
He says again, 'Good fences make good neighbors.'

A Bird, came down the Walk -
He did not know I saw -
He bit an Angle Worm in halves
And ate the fellow, raw,

And then, he drank a Dew
From a convenient Grass -
And then hopped sidewise to the Wall
To let a Beetle pass -

He glanced with rapid eyes,
That hurried all abroad -
They looked like frightened Beads, I thought,
He stirred his Velvet Head. -

Like one in danger, Cautious,
I offered him a Crumb,
And he unrolled his feathers,
And rowed him softer Home -

Than Oars divide the Ocean,
Too silver for a seam,
Or Butterflies, off Banks of Noon,
Leap, plashless as they swim.

Source: The Poems of Emily Dickinson: Reading Edition, edited by R.W. Franklin (Harvard University Press, 1999)

The instructor said,

> *Go home and write*
> *a page tonight.*
> *And let that page come out of you—*
> *Then, it will be true.*

I wonder if it's that simple?
I am twenty-two, colored, born in Winston-Salem.
I went to school there, then Durham, then here
to this college on the hill above Harlem.
I am the only colored student in my class.
The steps from the hill lead down into Harlem,
through a park, then I cross St. Nicholas,
Eighth Avenue, Seventh, and I come to the Y,
the Harlem Branch Y, where I take the elevator
up to my room, sit down, and write this page:

It's not easy to know what is true for you or me
at twenty-two, my age. But I guess I'm what
I feel and see and hear, Harlem, I hear you.
hear you, hear me—we two—you, me, talk on this page.
(I hear New York, too.) Me—who?

Well, I like to eat, sleep, drink, and be in love.
I like to work, read, learn, and understand life.
I like a pipe for a Christmas present,
or records—Bessie, bop, or Bach.
I guess being colored doesn't make me not like
the same things other folks like who are other races.
So will my page be colored that I write?
Being me, it will not be white.
But it will be
a part of you, instructor.
You are white—
yet a part of me, as I am a part of you.

That's American.
Sometimes perhaps you don't want to be a part of me.
Nor do I often want to be a part of you.
But we are, that's true!
As I learn from you,
I guess you learn from me—
although you're older—and white—
and somewhat more free.

This is my page for English B.

"Hope" is the thing with feathers -
That perches in the soul -
And sings the tune without the words -
And never stops - at all -

And sweetest - in the Gale - is heard -
And sore must be the storm -
That could abash the little Bird
That kept so many warm -

I've heard it in the chillest land -
And on the strangest Sea -
Yet - never - in Extremity,
It asked a crumb - of me.

Source: The Poems of Emily Dickinson Edited by R. W.
Franklin (Harvard University Press, 1999)

Well, son, I'll tell you:
Life for me ain't been no crystal stair.
It's had tacks in it,
And splinters,
And boards torn up,
And places with no carpet on the floor—
Bare.
But all the time
I'se been a-climbin' on,
And reachin' landin's,
And turnin' corners,
And sometimes goin' in the dark
Where there ain't been no light.
So boy, don't you turn back.
Don't you set down on the steps
'Cause you finds it's kinder hard.
Don't you fall now—
For I'se still goin', honey,
I'se still climbin',
And life for me ain't been no crystal stair.

Source: The Collected Works of Langston Hughes
(University of Missouri Press (BkMk Press), 2002)

A free bird leaps
on the back of the wind
and floats downstream
till the current ends
and dips his wing
in the orange sun rays
and dares to claim the sky.

But a bird that stalks
down his narrow cage
can seldom see through
his bars of rage
his wings are clipped and
his feet are tied
so he opens his throat to sing.

The caged bird sings
with a fearful trill
of things unknown
but longed for still
and his tune is heard
on the distant hill
for the caged bird
sings of freedom.

The free bird thinks of another breeze
and the trade winds soft through the sighing trees
and the fat worms waiting on a dawn bright lawn
and he names the sky his own

But a caged bird stands on the grave of dreams
his shadow shouts on a nightmare scream
his wings are clipped and his feet are tied
so he opens his throat to sing.

The caged bird sings
with a fearful trill

of things unknown
but longed for still
and his tune is heard
on the distant hill
for the caged bird
sings of freedom.

Source: The Complete Collected Poems of Maya Angelou
(Random House Inc., 1994)

**Ox Cart Man**
BY DONALD HALL

In October of the year,
he counts potatoes dug from the brown field,
counting the seed, counting
the cellar's portion out,
and bags the rest on the cart's floor.

He packs wool sheared in April, honey
in combs, linen, leather
tanned from deerhide,
and vinegar in a barrel
hooped by hand at the forge's fire.

He walks by his ox's head, ten days
to Portsmouth Market, and sells potatoes,
and the bag that carried potatoes,
flaxseed, birch brooms, maple sugar, goose
feathers, yarn.

When the cart is empty he sells the cart.
When the cart is sold he sells the ox,
harness and yoke, and walks
home, his pockets heavy
with the year's coin for salt and taxes,

and at home by fire's light in November cold
stitches new harness
for next year's ox in the barn,
and carves the yoke, and saws planks
building the cart again.

Source: Old and New Poems (1990)

**The Black Walnut Tree**
By Mary Oliver

My mother and I debate:
we could sell
the black walnut tree

to the lumberman,
and pay off the mortgage.
Likely some storm anyway
will churn down its dark boughs,
smashing the house. We talk
slowly, two women trying
in a difficult time to be wise.
Roots in the cellar drains,
I say, and she replies
that the leaves are getting heavier
every year, and the fruit
harder to gather away.
But something brighter than money
moves in our blood—an edge
sharp and quick as a trowel
that wants us to dig and sow.
So we talk, but we don't do
anything. That night I dream
of my fathers out of Bohemia
filling the blue fields
of fresh and generous Ohio
with leaves and vines and orchards.
What my mother and I both know
is that we'd crawl with shame
in the emptiness we'd made
in our own and our fathers' backyard.
So the black walnut tree
swings through another year
of sun and leaping winds,
of leaves and bounding fruit,
and, month after month, the whip-
crack of the mortgage.

*Source: Mary Oliver, New and Selected Poems, Volume 1,
Beacon Press, 2005.*

Now, the Star-Belly Sneetches-
Had bellies with stars.
The Plain-Belly Sneetches-Had none upon thars.
Those stars weren't so big. They were really so small.
You might think such a thing wouldn't matter at all.
But, because they had stars, all the Star-Belly Sneetches
Would brag, "We're the best kind of Sneetch on the
beaches.
With their snoots in the air, they would sniff and they'd
snort
"We'll have nothing to do with the Plain-Belly sort!"
And whenever they met some, when they were out walking,
They'd hike right on past them without even talking.
When the Star-Belly children went out to play ball,
Could a Plain- Belly get in the game...? Not at all.
You only could play if your bellies had stars
And the Plain-Belly children had none upon thars.
When the Star-Belly Sneetches had frankfurter roasts
Or picnics or parties or marshmallow toasts,
They never invited the Plain-Belly Sneetches.
They left them out cold, in the dark of the beaches.
They kept them away. Never let them come near.
And that's how they treated them year after year.
Then ONE day, seems...while the Plain-Belly Sneetches
Were moping and doping alone on the beaches,
Just sitting there wishing their bellies had stars...
A stranger zipped up in the strangest of cars!
"My friends," he announced in a voice clear and keen,
"My name is Sylvester McMonkey McBean.
And I've heard of your troubles. I've heard you're unhappy.
But I can fix that. I'm the Fix-it-Up Chappie.
I've come here to help you. I have what you need.
And my prices are low. And I work at great speed.
And my work is one hundred per cent guaranteed!
Then, quickly Sylvester McMonkey McBean
Put together a very peculiar machine.
And he said, "You want stars like a Star-Belly Sneetch...?

My friends, you can have them for three dollars each!"
"Just pay me your money and hop right aboard!"
So they clambered inside. Then the big machine roared
And it klonked. And it bonked. And it jerked. And it berked
And it bopped them about. But the thing really worked!
When the Plain-Belly Sneetches popped out, they had

stars!

They actually did. They had stars upon thars!
Then they yelled at the ones who had stars at the start,
"We're exactly like you! You can't tell us apart.
We're all just the same, now, you snooty old smarties!
And now we can go to your frankfurter parties."
"Good grief!" groaned the ones who had stars at the first.
"We're still the best Sneetches and they are the worst.
But, now, how in the world will we know," they all frowned,
"If which kind is what, or the other way round?"
Then came McBean with a very sly wink.
And he said, "Things are not quite as bad as you think.
So you don't know who's who. That is perfectly true.
But come with me, friends. Do you know what I'll do?
I'll make you, again, the best Sneetches on beaches
And all it will cost you is ten dollars eaches."
"Belly stars are no longer in style," said McBean.
"What you need is a trip through my Star-off Machine.
This wondrous contraption will take off your stars
So you won't look like Sneetches who have them on thars."
And that handy machine Working very precisely
Removed all the stars from their tummies quite nicely.
Then, with snoots in the air, they paraded about
And they opened their beaks and they let out a shout,
"We know who is who! Now there isn't a doubt.
The best kind of Sneetches are Sneetches without!"
Then, of course, those with stars all got frightfully mad.
To be wearing a star now was frightfully bad.
Then, of course, old Sylvester McMonkey McBean
Invited them into his star-off machine.
Then, of course from THEN on, as you probably guess,
Things really got into a horrible mess.
All the rest of that day, on those wild screaming beaches,

The fix-it-up Chappie kept fixing up Sneetches.
Off again! On Again! In again! Out again!
Through the machines they raced round and about again,
Changing their stars every minute or two.
They kept paying money. They kept running through
Until neither the Plain nor the Star-Bellies knew
Whether this one was that one...or that one was this one
Or which one was what one ...or what one was who.
Then, when every last cent
Of their money was spent,
The Fix-it-Up Chappie packed up
And he went.
And he laughed as he drove
In his car up the beach,
"They never will learn.
No. You can't teach a Sneetch!"
But McBean was quite wrong. I'm quite happy to say
That the Sneetches got really quite smart on that day,
The day they decided that Sneetches are Sneetches
And no kind of Sneetch is the best on the beaches
That day, all the Sneetches forgot about stars
And whether they had one, or not, upon thars.

Let America be America again.
Let it be the dream it used to be.
Let it be the pioneer on the plain
Seeking a home where he himself is free.

(America never was America to me.)

Let America be the dream the dreamers dreamed—
Let it be that great strong land of love
Where never kings connive nor tyrants scheme
That any man be crushed by one above.

(It never was America to me.)

O, let my land be a land where Liberty
Is crowned with no false patriotic wreath,
But opportunity is real, and life is free,
Equality is in the air we breathe.

(There's never been equality for me,
Nor freedom in this "homeland of the free.")

Say, who are you that mumbles in the dark?
And who are you that draws your veil across the stars?

I am the poor white, fooled and pushed apart,
I am the Negro bearing slavery's scars.
I am the red man driven from the land,
I am the immigrant clutching the hope I seek—
And finding only the same old stupid plan
Of dog eat dog, of mighty crush the weak.

I am the young man, full of strength and hope,
Tangled in that ancient endless chain
Of profit, power, gain, of grab the land!
Of grab the gold! Of grab the ways of satisfying need!
Of work the men! Of take the pay!

Of owning everything for one's own greed!

I am the farmer, bondsman to the soil.
I am the worker sold to the machine.
I am the Negro, servant to you all.
I am the people, humble, hungry, mean—
Hungry yet today despite the dream.
Beaten yet today—O, Pioneers!
I am the man who never got ahead,
The poorest worker bartered through the years.

Yet I'm the one who dreamt our basic dream
In the Old World while still a serf of kings,
Who dreamt a dream so strong, so brave, so true,
That even yet its mighty daring sings
In every brick and stone, in every furrow turned
That's made America the land it has become.
O, I'm the man who sailed those early seas
In search of what I meant to be my home—
For I'm the one who left dark Ireland's shore,
And Poland's plain, and England's grassy lea,
And torn from Black Africa's strand I came
To build a "homeland of the free."

The free?

Who said the free? Not me?
Surely not me? The millions on relief today?
The millions shot down when we strike?
The millions who have nothing for our pay?
For all the dreams we've dreamed
And all the songs we've sung
And all the hopes we've held
And all the flags we've hung,
The millions who have nothing for our pay—
Except the dream that's almost dead today.

O, let America be America again—
The land that never has been yet—

And yet must be—the land where every man is free.
The land that's mine—the poor man's, Indian's, Negro's, ME—
Who made America,
Whose sweat and blood, whose faith and pain,
Whose hand at the foundry, whose plow in the rain,
Must bring back our mighty dream again.

Sure, call me any ugly name you choose—
The steel of freedom does not stain.
From those who live like leeches on the people's lives,
We must take back our land again,
America!

O, yes,
I say it plain,
America never was America to me,
And yet I swear this oath—
America will be!

Out of the rack and ruin of our gangster death,
The rape and rot of graft, and stealth, and lies,
We, the people, must redeem
The land, the mines, the plants, the rivers.
The mountains and the endless plain—
All, all the stretch of these great green states—
And make America again!

Dreams
BY LANGSTON HUGHES

Hold fast to dreams
For if dreams die
Life is a broken-winged bird
That cannot fly.

Hold fast to dreams
For when dreams go
Life is a barren field
Frozen with snow.

I've got the children to tend
The clothes to mend
The floor to mop
The food to shop
Then the chicken to fry
The baby to dry
I got company to feed
The garden to weed
I've got shirts to press
The tots to dress
The cane to be cut
I gotta clean up this hut
Then see about the sick
And the cotton to pick.

Shine on me, sunshine
Rain on me, rain
Fall softly, dewdrops
And cool my brow again.

Storm, blow me from here
With your fiercest wind
Let me float across the sky
'Til I can rest again.

Fall gently, snowflakes
Cover me with white
Cold icy kisses and
Let me rest tonight.

Sun, rain, curving sky
Mountain, oceans, leaf and stone
Star shine, moon glow
You're all that I can call my own.

The Pool Players.
Seven at the Golden Shovel.

We real cool. We
Left school. We

Lurk late. We
Strike straight. We

Sing sin. We
Thin gin. We

Jazz June. We
Die soon.

Gwendolyn Brooks, "We Real Cool" from Selected Poems.
Copyright © 1963 by Gwendolyn Brooks. Reprinted with the
permission of the Estate of Gwendolyn Brooks. Source: Poetry
(1959)

Fire and Ice
BY ROBERT FROST

Some say the world will end in fire,
Some say in ice.
From what I've tasted of desire
I hold with those who favor fire.
But if it had to perish twice,
I think I know enough of hate
To say that for destruction ice
Is also great
And would suffice.

In a Station of the Metro
BY EZRA POUND

The apparition of these faces in the crowd:
Petals on a wet, black bough.

'Twas noontide of summer,
    And mid-time of night;
  And stars, in their orbits,
    Shone pale, thro' the light
Of the brighter, cold moon,
    'Mid planets her slaves,
Herself in the Heavens,
    Her beam on the waves.
      I gazed awhile
      On her cold smile;
Too cold- too cold for me-
    There pass'd, as a shroud,
    A fleecy cloud,
And I turned away to thee,
    Proud Evening Star,
    In thy glory afar,
And dearer thy beam shall be;
    For joy to my heart
    Is the proud part
Thou bearest in Heaven at night,
    And more I admire
    Thy distant fire,
Than that colder, lowly light.

The Cross of Snow
BY HENRY WADSWORTH LONGFELLOW

In the long, sleepless watches of the night,
  A gentle face — the face of one long dead —
  Looks at me from the wall, where round its head
  The night-lamp casts a halo of pale light.
Here in this room she died; and soul more white
  Never through martyrdom of fire was led
  To its repose; nor can in books be read
  The legend of a life more benedight.
There is a mountain in the distant West
  That, sun-defying, in its deep ravines
  Displays a cross of snow upon its side.
Such is the cross I wear upon my breast
  These eighteen years, through all the changing scenes
  And seasons, changeless since the day she died.

The Peace of Wild Things
BY WENDELL BERRY

When despair for the world grows in me
and I wake in the night at the least sound
in fear of what my life and my children's lives may be,
I go and lie down where the wood drake
rests in his beauty on the water, and the great heron feeds.
I come into the peace of wild things
who do not tax their lives with forethought
of grief. I come into the presence of still water.
And I feel above me the day-blind stars
waiting with their light. For a time
I rest in the grace of the world, and am free.

What happens to a dream deferred?

    Does it dry up
    like a raisin in the sun?
    Or fester like a sore—
    And then run?
    Does it stink like rotten meat?
    Or crust and sugar over—
    like a syrupy sweet?

    Maybe it just sags
    like a heavy load.

    Or *does it explode?*

What Kind of Times Are These
BY ADRIENNE RICH

There's a place between two stands of trees where the grass grows
uphill
and the old revolutionary road breaks off into shadows
near a meeting-house abandoned by the persecuted
who disappeared into those shadows.

I've walked there picking mushrooms at the edge of dread, but
don't be fooled
this isn't a Russian poem, this is not somewhere else but here,
our country moving closer to its own truth and dread,
its own ways of making people disappear.

I won't tell you where the place is, the dark mesh of the woods
meeting the unmarked strip of light—
ghost-ridden crossroads, leafmold paradise:
I know already who wants to buy it, sell it, make it disappear.

And I won't tell you where it is, so why do I tell you
anything? Because you still listen, because in times like these
to have you listen at all, it's necessary
to talk about trees.